The Manager's Balancing Act

The Manager's Balancing Act

Florence M. Stone

AMACOM
American Management Association

New York • Atlanta • Boston • Chicago • Kansas City • San Francisco • Washington, D.C.
Brussels • Mexico City • Tokyo • Toronto

This book is available at a special
discount when ordered in bulk quantities.
For information, contact Special Sales Department,
AMACOM, a division of American Management Association,
1601 Broadway, New York, NY 10019.

This publication is designed to provide accurate and authoritative
information in regard to the subject matter covered. It is sold with the
understanding that the publisher is not engaged in rendering legal,
accounting, or other professional service. If legal advice or other expert
assistance is required, the services of a competent professional person
should be sought.

Library of Congress Cataloging-in-Publication Data

Stone, Florence M.
    The manager's balancing act / Florence M. Stone.
        p.   cm.
    Includes bibliographical references and index.
    ISBN 0-8144-0374-3
    1. Management.   I. Title.
HD31.S6962   1997
658—dc21   97–2332
                                               CIP

Printing number

10   9   8   7   6   5   4   3   2   1

For
Mom...

Contents

Introduction

Recent management trends and developments hold great promise for more corporate creativity, improved communication, more collaboration and cooperation within organizations, and increased motivation and productivity. But they have also created problems for us as managers, problems that far outweigh many of their benefits.

I'm talking about teams and empowerment programs, value-driven performance appraisals; the first steps to virtual organizations; shared leadership; continuous change initiatives; the downsizings, which have created leaner, flatter, maybe more creative, organizations but also killed feelings of loyalty toward the organization; and creation of worknets, alliances, and partnerships with colleagues and the teams they lead.

Some of the resulting problems are directly undermining our own managerial productivity; others are eroding our employees' morale and thereby obstructing employee initiative; still others have created conflicts between us and our employees. Many can make a dramatic difference on our bottom line—which means they can make a dramatic impact on our careers.

Answers do not lie solely with the newest management techniques or thinking. Actually, some of the problems are a byproduct of the latest boardroom buzzwords. The answers, wryly, lie in blending the new ways of managing with traditional management. Doing this successfully is the *manager's balancing act*. It is a skill we managers must develop if we're to successfully use the best of the new.

There is much about traditional management that is time to

shelve. But not all traditional management techniques are obsolete. Much of traditional management is still applicable to today. And by applying these traditional techniques to today's work world, we can make the new practices of management truly effective, not simply passing fads that will do more harm than good. The secret lies in blending the best of management today with the best practices of management and leadership of the past. In blending the two, we will be better able to remotivate our burnt-out staffs, supervise more successfully off-site workers, create productive alliances with colleagues and partnerships between our team and theirs, cope with information overload from the new technology, make corporate values a reality in our operating areas, and successfully empower employees and share leadership.

As Shakespeare said, "Balance is all."

Tom Peters is correct that these are "crazy times," but to achieve the "wow" he writes about does not mean that we abdicate our responsibility for managing work. That's not what the new management means. Yes, the rules of the management game have changed—even the game has changed—but we players (think supervisors, managers, and team leaders) are still responsible for the work getting done. That means knowing how to manage in the new business climate and culture. Which means knowing which aspects of traditional management to apply to a situation to facilitate today's management.

In this book, I show you how you can control your own and your staff's productivity without forfeiting the creativity and other benefits that come from teaming and other characteristics of today's reorganized businesses. There are ten chapters in this book, but they reflect more than ten problems, as you'll see.

Each chapter has been divided into four sections. First, there is a description of the dysfunctional situation and related problems. If you doubt that issue is pertinent and wonder why you should care about it, you'll find in this section the answer to a question you likely ask yourself each time you pick up any management book: "What's In It for Me?," or "WIIFM."

Second, there is a discussion of those elements of conventional management relevant to the problem.

Next, there is a description of the newest developments either responsible for the situation or currently being used to resolve the dilemma. Where they aren't working or are exacerbating the situation, I explain why.

Fourth, and finally, you will read about the best solutions, many of which are based on recasting traditional management practices in today's environment. To share a simple example, many senior managements have set corporate values as a part of their strategic planning efforts in order to better direct the efforts of those below them. Several companies are asking their managers to use these as the basis for evaluations as well as for strategic and operational planning. But supervisors and managers alike are experiencing problems in appraisal interviews in using values to measure employee performance, even if the values have been promulgated to all within the organization. Disgruntled employees may go so far as to take their companies to court because of poor assessments that were based on expectations that were never communicated. But linking values to behavior, the basis for traditional performance evaluations and even Management by Objectives programs, clarifies expectations between a manager and her employees and eliminates the likelihood that an employee will contest the appraisal. Yet many companies have yet to tie values to behaviors. If you're skilled in the manager's balancing act, you can.

If you're a manager, you need this book to manage your workday, your staff meetings, and any cross-functional teams you lead; to build collaborative relationships with your colleagues; and otherwise to be successful in your job. If you doubt me, look at the twenty-five situations listed here. I expect you've encountered many yourself; if you haven't, you probably have heard about someone in your organization who has. They're the situations that continually frustrate and anger managers today. In this book, you'll discover the answers so that you can prevent their recurrence.

Situation 1. Jerry, a marketing manager, has been criticized for his directive management style by his boss, who expects Jerry to adapt his style to the company's more participative style. Helen, Jerry's assistant, is a nine-to-fiver, with little interest in career advancement, although she would like to earn more.

Should Jerry continue his directive style, which he's comfortable with, or empower Helen, even though she has made it clear that she doesn't want to be empowered? Is there some other option? (See Chapter 1.)

Situation 2. Pete's staff members are frustrated from being told to "work outside their boxes" yet continuously being reigned in when they do. What is Pete doing wrong? (See Chapter 1.)

Situation 3. Claire was given a major project by Bea as part of the company's effort to empower its employees and gain fully from their knowledge and ability. The project is due tomorrow, and Claire has just come to Bea to tell her that the project is running about a week behind schedule. She didn't want to let Bea know about the problems she was encountering because she didn't want to disappoint her. But now they both have a major problem. What did Bea do wrong? What should she say to Claire? (See Chapter 2.)

Situation 4. Sue is a supervisor in a plant, and she's worried now that her organization has reorganized around teams. Will she still have a job? What will be her role on and her responsibilities to these self-managed work teams? (See Chapter 2.)

Situation 5. There are rumors at Jed's organization that there will be layoffs. The company had layoffs a year ago, and morale has just begun to return to normal. Two employees have asked Jed if the rumors are true. Jed knows that they are but that they won't affect his department. What should he say to his staff? (See Chapter 3.)

Situation 6. Tim's department lost two of its eight employees in a downsizing last year. Morale and productivity are both down, so Tim is thinking of instituting an empowerment program and team effort to restore productivity. Are these the best solutions to the problem? (See Chapter 3.)

Situation 7. Carol's company downsized a few years ago, and employees are still talking about it; they expect the other shoe to fall any moment. The staff has lost two good workers to another company without a history of layoffs, and Carol doesn't want to lose other workers. How can she restore employee loyalty to the company? Will talking about how they are all members of the same team do it? (See Chapter 4.)

Situation 8. Stan has been talking to Jim about some training he should take to help him do his job better. Jim is enthusiastic, but he would also like to take some courses that have nothing to do with his job but could make him a better employee over the longer term—although not necessarily for Stan's company. Should Stan agree to let Jim take all the training he wants or limit him to only that course that will contribute to his job performance now? (See Chapter 4.)

Situation 9. Marty has a great idea about marketing her company's new software program to schools, but research is needed to ensure the success of the idea—and the research will cost. The company's red-tapers have refused. How can Marty get around the bureaucrats and get the funding that will make her marketing scheme a success? (See Chapter 5.)

Situation 10. Tim's been told to implement a new, more efficient way of processing customer orders, and he expects opposition from his staff. His boss, who is from the old school, has suggested that Tim just announce the change. But Tim knows he will need the cooperation of his reps for the idea to work. How can he get that cooperation and maintain staff motivation over the transition? (See Chapter 5.)

Situation 11. Darlene is buried under stacks of mail—paper and electronic—not to mention the many, many phone messages she must respond to. If she doesn't get some sense of control over all the information that comes over her desk, she knows she won't have time to do her job—which is identifying new products for her business. What can she do to deal with the information overload she finds every morning awaiting her? (See Chapter 6.)

Situation 12. Larry has found e-mail to be a real blessing. All those memos that he used to send on paper, he now sends electronically. But why doesn't he get responses? Could it be that the messages he's sending aren't getting through? Maybe he's pressing the wrong keys. Or do you think that he's sending the wrong kind of mail electronically? (See Chapter 6.)

Situation 13. Sid has noticed some looks between his team members when he speaks. Do you think that the team members don't think he's pulling his full weight? Maybe he should contribute more? It couldn't be that he always interrupts team members as they speak. After all, they take his apologies graciously. (See Chapter 6.)

Situation 14. Mildred is the team leader, and, as leader, she controls the discussion, even if it means raising and answering questions for the group to move them in the right direction. Is there another way? (See Chapter 6.)

Situation 15. Jim has called a meeting of his peers to discuss a proposal he wants to submit to his boss. He's already talked one-on-one with his peers about the proposal, and they are all enthusiastic. Jim needs one more piece of information, and he could call a colleague for that information and get it without holding a cross-functional team meeting, but all the management books advocate team product development. So Jim decides to bring together his peers in a meeting to discuss the idea one more time and get that last bit of information. Would you want to attend Jim's meeting if you were one of his peers? (See Chapter 7.)

Situation 16. Larry's company is into teaming, and Larry is willing to go along with the idea. So he institutes operational meetings of his direct reports. He plans to discuss a recurring problem during the first session. Larry arrives a few minutes late, announces that he hasn't had the time to prepare an agenda, and then begins, "The first issue I want to discuss is. . . ." How are these operating meetings getting off to the wrong start? (See Chapter 7.)

Situation 17. The team has agreed to price the new product at $129.95, but the marketing piece that was mailed says, "$159.95." When the team members learned about the change, they were furious. Marlene doesn't understand why they should be. After all, she is team leader and has the right to reverse a decision, doesn't she? (See Chapter 7.)

Situation 18. The company has promulgated a series of values to help employees focus strategically. To get buy-in, Hank's department has met twice to discuss the values. Each time, the employees have pointed to discrepancies between the values and norms within the organization. Hank agrees, but he doesn't think there is anything he can do about it. Is he right? (See Chapter 8.)

Situation 19. Barbara works for a company that has five values, and Barbara and her staff are familiar with these values. It's time to evaluate employees on these, but a problem has arisen. Barbara and Jim disagree as to whether he has demonstrated the value "Think globally." Barbara says he has done nothing to support the value, but Jim feels that his inclusion of some members of the overseas division in one of the work teams he runs, via audioconference, gets him off the hook. How could this disagreement have been avoided? (See Chapter 8.)

Situation 20. Todd and Marge had agreed to use a new process they had read about to move product more quickly from the plant's warehouse to the loading dock. But the shipments are still sitting in the warehouse. They call Kim, who heads up shipping, to complain. "Why didn't you move these along when they arrived?" Todd and Marge ask. "I didn't know they would be ready so soon," she answered. What did Todd and Marge forget in instituting all the plans to improve customer service? (See Chapter 9.)

Situation 21. Following a downsizing, Carl found himself having to merge the marketing department into the sales department he has headed for several years. The marketing staff is uneasy about the merger, and Carl's sales reps aren't any happier about having to share Carl's attention with the company's six marketing managers. What should Carl do immediately to resolve some of the unease? (See Chapter 9.)

Situation 22. Margaret's team needs to contact all the company's distributors to provide documentation to support an idea it has. Biff heads up market research but is adamant that his staff is too busy. "We've lost our secretary, and all my staff is too busy juggling the paperwork along with their routine jobs to help." What should Margaret suggest to get her team the help it needs? (See Chapter 9.)

Situation 23. Jake would like to get his production team to work more closely with engineering's group. He's met with Andy, the team head, and both agree that closer work relationships would help. But is it enough that only Jake and Andy talk regularly? What more can both team leaders do to encourage cooperation between the two groups? (See Chapter 9.)

Situation 24. Angie would like to work at home, and Grace, her supervisor, believes that the work can be done at home, but Grace hasn't said yes yet. Besides Angie's ability to do the work at home, what issues should Grace consider? (See Chapter 10.)

Situation 25. Jackie monitors her telemarketers via phone and manages by walking around. The company thinks that it can save considerably by off-siting the telemarketing effort. Can Jackie still get the productivity from her staff if she agrees to let them work at home? (See Chapter 10.)

If you want to solve these problems, you have to begin your balancing act. Which doesn't mean ignoring the new and different. Ideas don't become buzzwords unless there is worth to them. But to make them work, you need to go back to traditional management and take elements of it to create truly workable solutions. My goal is to help you understand what to do when faced with the dysfunctional situations of today and how to blend all the best of today and yesterday into solid solutions for effective management.

1

Should You Share Leadership?

Managers have been on a roller-coaster ride for some time now, and the ride is still not over. Companies will stay lean and flat, but they also will be looking for opportunities to grow their bottom lines—which means greater use of their human assets and increased employee participation in the management process.

There is much talk about empowerment today (see Chapter 2), but empowerment doesn't go far enough. Shared leadership means that employees not only have the challenge of making decisions about plans already set but making the plans themselves. We're talking about a new role for managers—as coaches and facilitators—in relationship to employees who independently or as members of self-directed work teams set mission and goals for their organization, following parameters set by senior management.

It's a wonderful opportunity for all.

After all, when an organization commits to shared leadership, it frees its managers to focus on new areas of growth for the business. The organization gets the benefit of the knowledge and insights that employees can bring to the work because they are closest to it.

And employees get a sense of control over their destinies, something that they likely feel they have lost in the waves of downsizing. Their jobs become more challenging. And they have the opportunity to develop new organizational and management skills, which could contribute to their employability and reestablish their commitment to the organization, which was lost when they recognized there was no such thing as job security, no matter how hard they worked.

The Problem

The mandate to shared leadership has frightened many managers, already suffering from change overload due to wave upon wave of downsizing, the introduction of new technology, restructuring and reorganization, and an assortment of other changes within the workplace. Stressed out, they see the move to self-directed work teams and greater employee participation in decision making as threats to their careers. Many companies have contributed to their feelings by instituting such initiatives without defining the new responsibilities of supervisors as team coaches or sponsors, or undertaking training of existing teams to prepare both the manager and members of the team for their new problem-solving responsibilities.

Change Overload

If you were looking for a word to describe the condition many managers are suffering from, it would be "change overload." As the silos in many companies have fallen and organizations have reorganized around teams, managers are scrambling to handle and implement the many changes in their jobs.

A major change seems to be occurring in the definition of leadership. Companies have to remember that the sharing of leadership by managers with those who were previously subordinates does not come easily—for either party.

Employees need training before they are fully ready for their new responsibility. Yes, some employees can handle shared leadership now, but many more will need time to understand all the issues they need to consider when they make a decision. Parameters, too, have to be set to help employees know when they can make decisions on their own and when they should go to their managers for advice. Otherwise, mistakes that could have been prevented will be made.

Managers who previously supervised in a more autocratic manner will need to learn a new way of managing. Just like their employees, managers have to understand what shared leadership entails.

Manager Overboard

Some managers have gone overboard, abdicating their supervisory responsibilities. In some cases, this is deliberate, a way to avoid making tough decisions. There are managers who hold meetings to make decisions that do not require the buy-in of employees or that could benefit from others' input, so staffs and managers waste considerable time in meetings that are unnecessary. These same managers, afraid to disagree with the group, accept the decisions of staff whether or not they are good ones.

In most instances, however, the problem is not that the manager is not afraid to make decisions but that the manager doesn't know how to truly communicate what shared leadership means.

Take Kathleen. She is in favor of shared leadership, and she has told her staff so. But, she wonders, does that mean that during slow times her employees should be allowed to socialize on the phone, play computer card games, read Ludlum novels, or sit around gossiping? That's what a visitor to the department would see. Of the seven people in her staff, only one seems to be working: Mike, a long-time employee with tremendous creativity, who is busy at his desk developing a proposal for a new way to handle incoming orders. Only he seems to understand the opportunity that shared leadership gives him to see his ideas implemented.

Kathleen believes that shared leadership can truly benefit her department. But in talking to her employees about their assuming responsibility for their work, somewhere along the line Kathleen didn't make it clear that they would continue to be accountable for performance. And Kathleen doesn't know how to remind them without coming across like a hypocrite about shared leadership.

Only on Paper

Hypocrites are what several employees tell me their bosses have become in talking the talk of shared leadership but not walking the walk. They complain that their managers use the "E" (for empowerment) and "T" (for teamwork) words, yet continue on their autocratic ways. Their organizations have mandated a shift, and these supervisors are going along with it but only in their communications to those below and above them. By nature autocratic in their management style, they worry that they won't fit into the new organization—and they are giving the trend lip service to delay the time that management gets wise to them.

But their actions—which we all know certainly speak louder than any of their words—are telling their employees that there will be no *real* change in the way the work is handled. The staff may sit in on meetings, but their manager (maybe here the right word is "boss") will still *tell* them what is to be done. If the workers are allowed to make a decision, the manager may feel comfortable reversing that decision without letting the group as a whole know why. If, on their own, employees try to handle problems without going to their boss, there will be repercussions when the boss finds out.

Managers like this see shared leadership as just another "flavor of the month," likely to disappear as companies settle down from the restructurings and get back to the business of making money. I think time will prove them wrong.

In the meantime, however, these managers' departments won't experience the boost in productivity that comes from shared leadership, but neither can they expect performance to be as before. Rather, morale is likely to decline and productivity to do the same as their employees realize that the promise of greater involvement in decisions—and more control over their destinies—is an empty promise for them.

Staffing Considerations

There may be some people on your staff who will never participate more than they do right now, like May, who is a nine-to-fiver and more concerned about her pay envelope than any challenges associated with the job, or Dan, who is better at doing the simpler tasks in your department.

In time, you may have to decide if the Mays and the Dans have a place in your new organization. But, as of now, efforts to involve them in decisions tend to come to naught as they sit sullenly in meetings contributing little or nothing to the discussions.

The Unconvinced Team

Some managers who have managed autocratically in the past but are willing to change may encounter another problem—staff skepticism. Irene is such a manager. She believes, as does her senior management, that shared leadership can lead to some significant improvements in operations—better and more creativity, significant cost savings, and improved productivity. Although she developed her managerial skills in a more authoritarian workplace, she is willing to make a dramatic change in her management style to achieve these objectives. The problem is that her staff just doesn't believe her.

Until now, in her role as sales manager, Irene has made all the decisions. And her past track record has come to haunt her. She has talked the talk but has yet to have an opportunity to walk the walk because none of her employees has taken the chance as yet because of her reputation.

When management sent the first in a series of memos to staff about the move to self-directed work teams, Irene met with her staff and explained her intention to support fully the program. "Well, that's that," she thought. "I hope it succeeds. It means more time for me to devote to some projects I have wanted to work on for some time."

But to Irene's dismay, there has been no change. Her administrative staff and reps continue to bring their problems to her to solve. She now holds regular meetings, but she finds the periods of silence deafening. Leaving one meeting, Randi, a long-time sales rep, said to her coworker, "After all these years, Irene suddenly decides we have brains. She's just waiting for the first mistake to prove the program won't work in sales." "Yeah, she's just going along with senior management on this. If we do something she disagrees with," said Hal, "she'll yell her head off, then reverse the decision, just like that time. . . ," and he recounted one of the many times that Irene had, indeed, stepped in and countermanded a decision.

WIIFM (What's In It for Me?)

You need to practice shared management—it is a natural progression from participative management—but you need to do it well—not only because of the benefits to your department and organization if you do.

In my earlier book, *The High-Value Manager*, which I co-authored with Randi T. Sachs, I observed how "high-value managers have learned how sharing their power gives them the time to work on high-visibility projects, to identify and pursue opportunities for their operation or company as a whole, and consequently to *increase their worth in the eyes of senior management.*" What makes a "high-value manager"? A high-value manager is someone who not only brings to her job critical skills, abilities, and knowledge but, more important in this context, is a manager who is highly valued by her company. Sharing leadership is a competency of the 1990s that organizations value.

Fighting the mandate tooth and nail will likely get you singled out—*but,* as someone who no longer fits within the corporate culture. And giving lip service to the change while practicing just the opposite style of management only erodes employee morale and levels of performance. If your department has bottom-line responsibility, it could result in your staff members becoming so demoralized that you don't make budget— which could mean further downsizing within your department.

If you think you already practice shared leadership, take this test to confirm it. The more yes replies, the more you practice shared leadership. Even if you score 100 percent, you should continue to read on. Check out "The Balancing Act" to be sure that you are doing all you can to make shared leadership work.

- When you are away from the office, do you feel assured that the office will run well without you?

- Do you ask your team members for ideas about changes that are needed and work with them to apply their suggestions?
- Do you incorporate members' suggestions as you work together to determine operating principles and procedures?
- Do you anticipate the information and other resources staff members will need and work to get it for them?
- Do you listen to an employee's concerns about an assignment, then help him or her think through the steps that need to be taken?
- Do you encourage everyone on your staff to talk informally about new ideas and ways of organizing or thinking about an issue?
- Do you run the kinds of meetings in which staff feel encouraged to talk about issues, express ideas, and thoughts with every person?
- Do you try to encourage exchanges of information between staff members and between your staff members and others within the organization without your being present?
- Do you praise your group for looking at problems outside its responsibilities and offering solutions?
- Do you encourage your staff members to learn new skills that will free them to make more and better decisions without you?
- Must you tell each employee what to do?
- Must you read every document that leaves the department?
- Do those who report to you have the authority to move work they've done along to an internal or external customer without your approval?

Back to the Basics

In the past, a boss was a boss. He gave workers orders, and they followed them. A manager was measured by his ability to plan, control, and organize work. Management was the act of getting work done by others. This is still true. But motivational research has changed the way we think that goal can be most productively accomplished.

Before the work of Abraham Maslow, David C. McClelland, and others, how motivated employees were about doing their work wasn't even an issue. Employees either did the work they were assigned or they didn't, and if they didn't, they were fired. But the research into what motivates individuals showed that employees would work harder and produce more under certain circumstances. This observation led to further research to correlate leadership styles to employee motivation.

How to Motivate Employees

Managers found themselves responsible for finding ways to motivate employees or, as research later discovered, creating a work environment in which employees would feel motivated; further studies into motivation discovered that a manager couldn't motivate an employee but, rather, could create the kind of environment that would encourage employees to want to work harder. Still other studies showed how leadership style could increase motivation and thereby raise productivity.

Of the studies done, those most relevant are the studies that support the wisdom of selecting a style most suitable for the individuals and situation involved. Among these is Dr. Fred Fiedler's contingency or situational leadership approach, which argues that a manager will be successful in a particular situation only if three factors are in balance: (1) the positive feelings between supervisor and supervised, (2) the kind of work to be done, in terms of how carefully procedures have to be followed, and (3) the amount of real authority the employee has over the assignment.

The Leadership Continuum

Perhaps more appropriate than Fiedler's work to today's move to shared leadership is the work of Rensis Likert, however. Likert identified a continuum of four leadership systems:

1. Exploitative autocratic style. Exploitative autocrats make all the decisions about what is to be done, how it is to be done, and who is to do it. Failure to follow instructions leads to punishment. Communication is downward, from manager to employee, and there is little trust between the supervisor and the worker.

2. Benevolent autocratic style. These managers and supervisors still make the decisions, but they deal more kindly with their employees, treating them more like children than the adults they are.

3. Democratic style. These supervisors seek workers' opinions and ideas before either making decisions or setting goals, but the managers make the final decision. Still, there is two-way communication, which is an improvement over the autocratic styles.

4. Participative style. Participative supervisors involve workers in setting goals and making decisions. They share information freely and encourage discussion. Employees have control over how the work is done, and trust exists between staff members and managers.

Likert's research went on to show that companies are most successful in implementing participative management when there is a commitment to employee participation at all levels, open communication, trust between staff members and management, respect for one another's knowledge, supportive relationships, group problem solving, and work autonomy. But it also found that some situations lend themselves to participative management whereas others do not. In general, a participative style proves successful when workers are familiar with corporate goals and are committed to their success, want to share responsibility for decision making, and bring knowledge of the work to the situation.

It is interesting that employee morale was found to decline—and productivity subsequently also to fall—when employees expected a participative leadership style but did not get one.

Likert found that participative management doesn't motivate if employees are less responsible, committed, or experienced. Then a more authoritarian style is needed. There are also situations that lend themselves to either authoritarian or democratic styles rather than to the participative style. The technology, time pressure, and nature of the work or decision are all factors to be considered in using participative management.

Although initial reaction in the 1960s to the idea of participative management, like that to the drive for shared leadership today, was fear—managers thought that participative management would weaken their authority to get the work done—Likert found that participative management was the most productive way to manage.

In examining all four of his styles, it might be best to picture them as points on a continuum of styles. At one extreme, a supervisor or manager has complete authority; at the other, employees share leadership and have tremendous freedom. Between the extremes are an infinite number of points, each reflecting different mixtures of the two extremes.

Strategic Management/Leadership

Writing in the magazine *Supervisory Management*, Oliver Niehouse, a trainer/consultant and president of Niehouse & Associates, described an approach called Strategic Management that reflects the thinking behind the continuum—and likely addresses our need today for an approach to shared leadership that reflects even more the relationship between leadership style and situation. Niehouse speaks about linking leadership style to the maturity and knowledge of the employee and the task involved (see Figure 1). Style 1 (S1) is a very directive style, with the focus on doing the task as told (high task) and little relationship building (low relationship). Style 2 (S2) is also a very directive leadership style (high task) but in a more persuasive, guiding manner (high relationship). A style 3 (S3) manager is less directive (low task) and solicits more input from the employee, consequently calling for a more collaborative style (high relationship). And a style 4 (S4) manager uses a delegating style of leadership behavior that is low task and low relationship.

Figure 1. Follower's level of readiness.

Style 3 (S3) low task high relationship	**Style 2** (S2) high task high relationship
Style 4 (S4) low task low relationship	**Style 1** (S1) high task low relationship

high ↑ Relationship Behavior ↓ low

low ← Task Behavior → high

high	moderate		low
R4	R3	R2	R1

Niehouse added a third element—the employee's readiness and level of competence, as well as willingness to assume responsibility and have commitment. R1s have little skill and low willingness; R2s have little skill and some willingness but low commitment; R3s have strong skills, some insecurity, and high commitment; and R4s have strong skills, confidence, and commitment.

Niehouse contended that with this basic knowledge, a manager could select an appropriate style of leadership for a given situation and employee using these simple steps.

First, a manager would determine the task. Next, she would determine the follower's level of readiness for the task; the manager would then match the readiness to the same numbered leadership style. Thus, an R1 readiness calls for an S1 style of leadership, R2 for S2, and so on.

Remember Kathleen, who is sharing leadership with her staff but running into some staff performance problems? This paradigm might explain her problem if you think about her staff. On the basis of his work experience and his commitment to his job, Mike is a highly capable R4. So he fits well into a shared leadership program. Of Kathleen's remaining six workers, four are relatively new to the company. They are R1s or R2s, at best, and need more leadership for now. Two are R3s, so with time Kathleen can prepare them for shared leadership by building on their high commitment.

Kathleen thought all her employees were ready for shared leadership. Not so. Her failure to understand this led to the party atmosphere in her department. Even with a complete staff of Mikes, however, shared leadership does not mean that a manager can abdicate her leadership role. But while underleadership has a negative effect on productivity, overleadership is the more destructive. If you put yourself in the shoes of employees who have been promised shared leadership and welcomed the offer but found the promise to be empty, you can understand the plummeting productivity in departments where empowerment programs have proven to be words with little substance. Generally, in such instances employees become frustrated and exasperated to the point that they leave. If they can't leave, they attempt to get even in the form of malicious obedience.

Fad Solutions

Shared leadership has taken the form of self-directed work teams in many plants. Even the most traditional organizations are increasing team activity—under the assumption, I suppose, that this is the easiest way to involve employees in decision making.

In manufacturing plants, supervisors and managers who have yet to accept or truly understand their new responsibility as coaches may discourage employees from working in teams by failing to make available to them the resources they need to see their ideas succeed; they may fail to communicate information to team members that is critical to their accomplishing their objectives; or they may become hypercritical of team decisions, undermining the self-confidence of employees undertaking their first managerial steps.

In more traditional organizations, the mandate has called for greater participation of employees in decision making, which has led to increased team activity.

Managerial Mistakes

In leading teams, there are four mistakes that managers make in trying to share leadership.

First, rather than provide direction for teams whose members are new or unfamiliar with their tasks, they overcontrol, dominating the team sessions. As much a problem are the many managers who overinvolve employees, holding meetings to get staff input where it is uncalled for; staff members focus on issues to which they can't contribute and are distracted from their day-to-day work, where they can truly make a contribution.

A third mistake some managers make is overaccommodating teams, letting team discussions go on without alerting members to the fact that they might be moving in the wrong direction. Barney is coach of several self-directed work teams. Previously a supervisor at this Boston-based plant, he has learned that you can't just sit like a statue when you hear the team moving out of range of its mission or purpose. You may not be its supervisor anymore, or even the team leader, but it is important that you speak up, call time out, and ask the team if it is still on the right track. Coaches aren't coaches if they agree with anything the team comes up with, bending over backwards to be supportive even when the team's initiative is inappropriate or its recommendations make no sense.

Finally, there are team leaders who walk away from team members and the team's objectives and provide no advice or counsel or help in getting needed resources. They may even go so far as not to attend team meetings. In essence, they abdicate responsibility for achieving the team's goal. They've given up leadership entirely.

Thinking Outside the Box

Managers have begun to use a new phrase: "Think outside your box." By this, the managers mean that employees should begin to identify and pursue opportunities beyond those within their job description. This can mean great opportunities for organizations. Without clear direction, however, the admonition usually ends up causing a situation like the one that Don was in.

Don is a sales rep with a print house. Sam, the head of the company, is also the chief marketing executive, and he's read all the books on shared leadership. An entrepreneur himself, he generally appreciates entrepreneurial thinking when he sees it in others.

So when he read about the value in getting employees to look beyond their jobs for opportunities, he thought it was a great idea. At the next staff meeting, which included all the sales reps, he made a point of encouraging each of the group's members to begin to search outside their jobs for opportunities for the company.

Sam didn't become the president of his own business because of lack of sales ability. He left each of those in the room eager to get out and identify those great ideas that could lead to significant growth for the company.

This story would likely be a better one if I could tell you that all seven of the individuals came back with a great idea. Unfortunately, I can't. Only six of the seven people in the room did come with some new way of saving money or making money that Sam loved and asked them to pursue.

The problem was with Don's idea. He had met with a small print shop that had been doing a fair amount of handbill printing, something Sam's company had considered and quickly dropped as insignificant, given the start-up costs and rep time. But Don learned that this printer was considering giving up his business, and without talking to Sam—after all, Sam had said that he wanted the staff to think for itself—Don came close to making a deal to buy the printer's business.

I know Sam well, and I can tell you that hearing Don tell his story almost gave him a stroke. "I tried to stay calm," he told me, recounting the tale, "but how can you stay calm when you hear one of your sales reps cavalierly announce that he may have just committed you to a $100,000 purchase of a business you don't want? I'm afraid I used words that my mother would wash my mouth out with soap for using, if she were alive," he told me. "Don has a temper, and he just walked out. It's a pity. He's a good salesman—just not too bright up here," Sam said, pointing to his head.

"What about the other ideas from the meeting?" I asked.

"They were fine. Each person looked into his work area or sales territory and came back with something I can use. But Don's idea—whew, thank God he didn't have a pen or I'd be in the handbill business."

What I didn't want to tell Sam that night—it would have given him apoplexy—was that he was responsible for what happened to Don. Don did exactly what Sam had told him—he looked outside his box, which is selling printing to various organizations, and he thought he had a wonderful business venture for the company. The problem was that Sam never explained to Don how far outside the box he should have been looking—or, at least, at what point he should have come back with the idea to discuss it with Sam.

This isn't the only problem I've come upon, either, with exhorting employees to look outside the box (or "color outside the lines," an alternative phrase for the same idea). The other, equally bad problem is that employees, particularly very creative ones, get so wrapped up in looking outside their boxes that they forget to do the work within the boxes. Operating problems occur because they are chasing opportunities that might or might not pan out, to the disruption of their routine work.

The Balancing Act

Before we even get to the balancing act, let me be perfectly honest. Whereas the threats earlier managers saw in participative management did not occur, there may be real reason to worry about shared leadership. The move in this direction may, indeed, lead to further downsizings in certain organizations.

As one manager pointed out to me, as plants reorganize around teams, there will be a need for coaches but fewer coaches than the number of supervisors previously needed, since one coach may oversee several teams. So the loss of supervisory jobs is very possible in companies that move toward self-directed work teams.

Those supervisors and managers who find it impossible to work within the new workplace will have to begin looking elsewhere to find more traditional supervisory responsibilities. In *The High-Value Manager*, I advocate that every manager have a Career Plan B at all times (under "Life Skills"). If you find the idea of sharing accountability with staff impossible to accept or believe that you may find yourself among those let go as your organization moves more firmly into a team structure, then take out your pen or pencil and begin thinking in terms of future career opportunities.

But do remember this: Having talked to several supervisors who are now team coaches, I know that the responsibilities one takes on as team coach are challenging and exciting. Coaches are team facilitators, part-time trainers, negotiators for resources, tacticians, and part-time human resources managers, as well as team cheerleaders and storytellers (of team lore to sustain team spirit during bad times).

That said, let me tell you that shared leadership involves a balancing act that will require you to utilize traditional leadership skills from the old command and control structure and apply them to the new ideas of teamwork and empowerment. Whether you are sharing leadership in a traditional organization or in one organized around teams, your first steps are to:

• *Examine your natural leadership style.* Ask yourself if you are by nature or circumstance autocratic directive, benevolent directive, democratic, or participative. If you are autocratic, can you do more than give lip service to shared leadership?

• *Analyze those individuals on your staff or in the self-directed work team you lead or coach.* Use the Strategic Management technique to measure which of your employees are ready for greater involvement in decision making and which aren't. Identify, too, who could be ready with some training. Do you think it wouldn't hurt if you took a course as well to make you a better team facilitator or participative leader?

• *Ask yourself if you are adapting your approach to shared leadership on the basis of the people and tasks involved.* Keep in mind the traditional management theory about motivation and leadership. Allow your management/leadership style to reflect the situation, skills, or experience of the individual and task involved.

• *Ask yourself if you are abdicating decision-making authority within a team or as staff leader.* The trend toward consensus-driven decision making is causing managers and supervisors to question when they can make independent decisions. Don't forget: Not all decisions need to be made within a team setting by the entire team. There are decisions that are more efficiently or effectively made by you even within the team, provided you have made it clear to the team or staff from the first day you met as a group that you will occasionally act unilaterally.

That there is nothing wrong with a leader who makes the final decision even within a team structure is evident from the reaction of managers and employees alike to the television (and now movie) character of Jean-Luc Picard, captain of the Starship *Enterprise* (think "team leader" or "manager") from the sci-fi show *Star Trek: The Next Generation.* The show had yet to hit the movie theaters when a trainer I know, who continues to be a fan of the show, told me, "He is the kind of leader most managers would like to believe they are."

Managers see in Jean-Luc a participative leader, someone who brings his direct reports together to discuss their options, listens *empathically* to their ideas, then decides on the option that he believes has the best chance of success. He doesn't get drawn into the details. He empowers his crew to carry out the plan he has chosen with three words that have become familiar to every fan of the show and have even become the basis for (would you believe?) a management book: *"Make It So."*

• *Don't overinvolve your employees.* Meetings can be productive for identifying problems, clarifying goals, generating alternatives, choosing the best solution, building an action plan, and monitoring implementation. Sometimes you will be seeking input but making the final decision yourself; other times it will be a group call. But these are the reasons for holding meetings, not to demonstrate to everyone within the organization that you have bought into the shared leadership theory.

- *Encourage employees to believe in their potential and capabilities.* Help them before problem solving meetings to see the opportunities there. Get them to look on problems as challenges and to recognize their ability to master them.

- *Talk to employees about what you expect of them.* If shared leadership represents a significant change in the way you manage, then you need to let your employees know that you are endeavoring to change and to ask for their support and patience. The adjustments for both of you will not be easy.

Hold a staff meeting in which you explain to your employees how you want to change your management style. Be honest, and point out that the organization is changing not only for the employees' benefit but for its own.

- *Reward employees who make independent decisions.* If you can't provide financial rewards, look for challenging assignments that will give them an opportunity to demonstrate their capabilities.

- *Lead or sponsor productive teams.* If your organization isn't organized around self-directed work teams and a problem arises, encourage your employees to work together and to form teams with workers from other areas to address the problem.

- *Facilitate a culture that encourages shared leadership.* Work to establish values that encourage employees to operate outside their boxes. Encourage, guide, and reward employees who display self-leadership while continually demonstrating your own leadership.

- *Clarify what you mean by "work outside your box."* Don't get so enthusiastic about the buzzphrase that you forget what it can cost you—like routine work not done as an employee chases moonbeams that have nothing to do with the strategic direction of the organization or wastes valuable time on an effort with no real return.

2

Making Empowerment Programs Work

Empowerment does not go so far in sharing your authority with employees as does shared leadership (see Chapter 1). Still, many managers have problems empowering their employees. There is also confusion about what empowerment means.

I was recently in a group meeting in which the topic of empowerment arose. "A new buzzword for delegation," Millie said sarcastically. "Not at all," said Bea. "Empowerment is very different from delegation."

The conversation was interesting in two ways. First, it was interesting because it revealed the confusion about what empowerment truly entails. And, second, it was interesting because Bea's and Millie's responses revealed their distinctly different styles of management—Bea, who was more participative and Millie, who tended to be authoritarian—and may explain why Millie is always complaining that she has too little time to focus on her own work because she's always doing her employees' jobs.

A Buzzword of the 1990s

Empowerment has been gaining currency in management circles as more and more companies move to employee involvement. Millie was right when she referred to it as one of the more popular new words in business vocabularies. But so was Bea: Empowerment is not just another word for delegation.

When we delegate a task to an employee, we are instructing that person to do the task for us. It's a responsibility we've given to another and can easily take from that person as supervisor if we like.

On the other hand, when we empower, we lower decision making to those who report to us. Empowerment represents authority that we allow others to share. We simply demonstrate our willingness to let employees share this through our management style, the work environment we create, and our positive response to those occasions when our employees use their power but make a mistake.

The last point is critical: When we empower, we can expect mistakes to happen; our responsibility, through coaching and training, is to minimize them.

Two Very Different Managers

Bea—Supporting True Empowerment

Bea empowers her employees. This is something she has had to learn. She once told me: "Don't think it isn't hard for me not to take over when a problem arises, because it is. To keep myself from doing so, I may even have to physically walk away from a situation, maybe even visit the employee lounge for awhile or a colleague, anything rather than be where my employees can ask me what to do." But, she added, "Over time, I've learned that I can trust my employees to make decisions on their own. They have guidelines that I've given them to provide some help. I've given them training to prepare them for the tough problems that may come their way. And I've spent time helping them to understand corporate finance so they appreciate the implications of any decision they make. And," she continued, "they know I am always there for moral support if they make the wrong decision."

Giving her employees the authority to operate independently on most issues means that Bea has more time to handle the responsibilities that have come from her participation in a number of critical corporate projects.

Recently, Bea had to prove that she was doing more than giving lip service to empowerment. She was at a meeting that was expected to last all day when the design for a new catalog came in. The production department insisted on immediate turnaround of the proofs to ensure delivery on schedule. Bea's copywriter and administrative assistant looked over the catalog, identified some errors that needed correction, reviewed the colors chosen by production, and finally OK'd the catalog themselves rather than wait for Bea, who wouldn't be back in the office until after 4:30. If they had waited for Bea, the catalog would not have gone back to the printer until the next day, and its distribution would have been delayed at least a week because of the printer's work schedule.

When Bea returned, she was told what had happened. Looking at the copy of the proofs that her staff had made for her, Bea, a twenty–year veteran of marketing, found several other changes she would have wanted made to the catalog. What did she say to her employees? Nothing.

Several weeks later, when the first samples of the catalog were received, Bea brought them to a staff meeting. There, she commended the designer and production manager for the overall design *and* her copywriter and assistant for ensuring that the catalog went out on schedule. Holding the catalog for a moment or two, she then said, "You know, next time let's see if we can add a place on the coupon for customers to fill out their e-mail numbers." Then, she continued, "What do you think of this opening page for the targeted market?"

She made the meeting into a training session, helping to prepare her copywriter, assistant, and others on her staff so that, the next time, they would be aware of these other issues as well.

Millie—Retaining Control

Millie would argue that she, too, practices empowerment, but those who work for her know otherwise.

Millie holds team meetings in which she raises questions for the group, pauses, then proceeds to answer them herself. There's no question she is in charge. She's been known to give assignments to her employees, then take them back when an employee reports that he or she has done something differently from the way Millie would do it. Millie doesn't mind empowering someone, but her definition of empowerment is giving employees the power to do the work *exactly* as she wants it done. Which is not what empowerment is about. Remember, when you empower, you tell the worker what needs to be done but you leave it to the worker to decide how to do it.

Millie is always complaining about how little time she has to devote to her work, but then she is so busy making decisions for her employees and responding to their questions about what they should do next that she has little time for her own responsibilities. Certainly she has little time for the high-visibility projects Bea is involved in.

The Problem

The problem with empowerment when it is practiced as Millie practices it is that it demoralizes and builds resentment, rather than increasing productivity and creativity, which is what successful empowerment efforts can do. Unfortunately, too many empowerment efforts resemble Millie's. They are designed more to make employees feel like they have input than to give them input—and this ploy usually backfires. Instead of motivating, the empowerment effort demotivates.

Managers use the "E" word and promise to let employees be free to make decisions. But as soon as an employee tries to make a decision, the manager intervenes.

The Issue of Competence

A common problem with many empowerment programs occurs when a manager does step away from a situation to let an employee handle it on his own but fails to prepare the employee beforehand for her new responsibility.

That's what happened to Darla.

A customer rep, Darla had learned from Ralph, a buyer, that his company would be interested in consolidating all its stationery purchases. If Darla could develop a package that made a strong case for Ralph's using her company to supply his company with all its stationery, her organization could perhaps land a big contract.

Darla knew that the deal would represent a real coup for her company. The opportunity would be lost if she didn't act on the offer (the sales rep for Ralph's area was in the hospital, recovering from bypass surgery), so Darla decided to develop some prices for Ralph on the basis of her knowledge of competitors' prices and her own estimate about what would be fair.

She then prepared a price sheet and sent it to Ralph's company, which was delighted to see the discounts that Darla was offering. Ralph called Darla and told her to prepare the contract; his company would sign it as soon as it was received. His company was delighted with the deal being offered.

Fortunately, Darla was so pleased with her accomplishment that she ran to Juan's office to tell him what happened. Juan, the head of customer service, was as pleased as Darla with the likelihood of a major new account until he saw the prices that Darla was quoting. Then he nearly hit the roof. "How could you?" he asked. "These prices are 20 percent below our deepest discounts!"

"But I didn't know that," answered Darla, who was relatively new to the company. Frightened by Juan's manner, her voice began to quiver. "What should we do?" she asked.

"I'll have to call Ralph and let him know that there is no way we'll sell office supplies at these prices. We would be losing money on every shipment to his business—maybe as much as $15,000 in all."

Darla's face turned pale. "I'm sorry," she mumbled, her head down.

Juan continued, "This is what comes of letting employees make decisions that they aren't prepared to make."

I don't think I need to tell you that Darla thereafter didn't make any decisions without first checking with Juan; if it wasn't allowed in the policy manual, customers could just go elsewhere, as far as she was concerned—why get into hot water again on the chance of making a few extra dollars for the company? As a result, several other opportunities for major accounts never were realized.

What Darla couldn't ignore, she passed on to Juan—which made it hard for him to handle his own work.

If you think about what happened, it's evident that Darla was only trying to help a customer and her company. If anyone was at fault, it was Juan. He was right when he said, "This is what comes of letting employees make decisions that they aren't prepared to make." Darla wasn't prepared to handle this issue. Who was responsible for that? Juan.

I don't think that managers deliberately set their employees up to fail when they empower them. But too often they don't give them the skills, abilities, and knowledge they need to succeed, either. That's their role in empowering their employees. And it's an important one. They no longer control their employees, but they do lead and support them.

For those managers who worry that empowerment is a threat to their position, let me emphasize that by giving your employees the power to do more, to assist you in doing your job better, you ultimately will gain time both to handle your own responsibilities and to take a greater leadership role in your organization.

WIIFM

When you empower your employees, you benefit from a highly motivated staff. Employees are inspired to work harder when they are given more control over their work. Empowered, they are energized, eager to identify ways to help both their company and the supervisor who is empowering them. That is you.

Have you ever wondered why an employee who can come up with an idea to increase sales at a church social or who has the organizational ability to put together a high school reunion doesn't seem able to think or act independently on the job? A major reason is that the employee hasn't been given a reason to do so.

Empowering the employee provides the reason. When you empower your employees, they are willing to take the initiative to improve the way their work is done. They see things that are being done inefficiently, and they can recommend more efficient methods. They share these ideas because, in empowering them, you have raised their level of concern about the company; they feel as if they have a share in its success.

Keep in mind how unempowered employees can behave: They offer little input and are insecure about making any decision, which means that they are in and out of your office daily to get confirmation of any decision that has to be made. They follow established guidelines, which is fine, but sometimes limiting someone to established guidelines makes him or her blind to the opportunities available. Or they make you unaware of problems. Unempowered employees think, "Since they won't listen to me, why should I bother trying to improve things?"

All right, Darla made a mistake, but what would have happened if Darla hadn't cared at all and let Ralph's query fall between the cracks?

If you don't empower your employees, instead of focusing attention on the opportunities to increase revenues or reduce costs, they will be concerned with only one thing—their pay. They will have no sense of ownership of their job. That comes only when they see their ideas being implemented. Look at what a difference empowerment had for Jill.

Jill considered her job dull. A purchasing agent, she did what she had to do and nothing more. When her boss told her that the company was implementing self-directed work teams as a part of a corporate cultural shift, Jill had her doubts. "It's just another way to get more work out of us," she thought.

Stan, her boss, was at the first meeting of Jill's team. He described the situation the team was formed to handle—the company wanted to set supplier vendor standards. Jill sat quietly and listened. "He's going to tell us what to do, and then we'll do it," she thought to herself.

But after describing the team's mission, Stan wished the group luck with its project and left.

There was some hesitation at first; then the group got down to work. Jill found herself becoming interested in what was being said. Suddenly she raised her hand. The group liked her idea. By the time the session had ended, Jill and the four other buyers had clarified their mission, set operating ground rules, and agreed on tasks they would complete by the next meeting.

If you want to know what supporting empowerment means to you (*what's in it for you* in supporting empowerment), the best person to ask is Stan, Jill's boss.

Jill's team got lots of recognition when it completed its project. And Stan shared indirectly in that recognition without having to take time away from some critical projects he was working on.

Back to the Basics

Employee empowerment and self-managed work teams grew out of the participative programs of the 1970s and 1980s. But empowerment programs take the participative programs much, much further. Today's empowerment programs involve employees not only in implementing decisions without supervisory direction but in making those decisions, whereas the earlier participative programs drew employees into only the implementation phase of procedural changes or other programs. And fewer programs did even this than the business press of the time seemed to suggest, with case studies of companies extolling employees' accomplishments.

The truth is that many of those early participative programs involved employees only in the sense that they were allowed to look on as others discussed the issues and made decisions. Those employees who were a part of these earlier programs frequently weren't prepared for discussion of the issues. Management's goal was not to increase the quality of the decisions being made by gaining input from those closest to the work problems but rather to increase employee job satisfaction by giving them a sense of involvement. These programs were the result of research by behaviorists Abraham Maslow and Frederick Herzberg, who argued for employee involvement as a means of increasing employee morale and thereby employee productivity.

No question, those programs that truly gave employees a

voice in decisions about new procedures or changes to existing operating guidelines truly generated high-performing teams. But those programs led by managers who let employees speak but were deaf to their ideas or who invited their employees to attend meetings but never called on them to hear their views only contributed to disgruntlement and cynicism about employee involvement.

Keep in mind: Employee involvement is designed to achieve greater results; it is not an end in itself. This was a big mistake in the participative and employee involvement efforts of the 1970s and 1980s and should not be repeated with the empowerment efforts of the 1990s.

Difficulties With Delegation

Besides these early participative efforts, any discussion about management basics related to empowerment has to include mention of delegation, not only because many people confuse it with empowerment—remember Millie—but also because both management techniques experience similar problems and can benefit from similar solutions.

Here's how delegation works: Your manager gives you a project to complete. You determine the tasks the project entails, and you assign various aspects of the job to your employees. If you are good at delegation, you give your employees some choice in how they do their part of the project. But when you delegate, you are still in control of the final work. You can take the assignment away from the employee if you have concerns about his or her ability to successfully complete the work.

Many of the concerns raised by managers who dislike to delegate are also raised about empowerment. They include:

- *Lack of trust.* Managers who don't delegate worry that their employees won't be able to do the job right. Better that they do it themselves and ensure that the work is done correctly.

- *Loss of control.* Another reason managers don't delegate is their fear that the employees to whom they delegate work won't do it as they would. And putting work in another's hands doesn't provide the same assurance that it will be completed on schedule as handling it yourself.

• *Fear of loss of position.* Some managers who refuse to delegate admit to a worry that an employee may show them up and take their job. They fear that the employee will demonstrate that she is better at doing the work than the supervisor; the supervisor doesn't want that to happen.

Sound similar to the reasons given for not empowering?

Delegation—Doing It Right

When managers measure their time savings from delegation— how it frees them to focus on their own tasks—they rethink their attitudes about delegation. To address their fears, they:

• *Set standards.* By making clear to employees their definition of quality, they increase the chances that the finished work will be satisfactory.

• *Train employees to handle the assignment.* They spend the time up front preparing their employees to take on the responsibilities they are to be delegated and to handle them well. Since assignments are generally task-oriented, the training is usually skill-based.

• *Build employee confidence.* Employees who have been the target of managers who dislike delegating often are unwilling to take on other assignments; after all, who would want to have someone hovering over his shoulder and criticizing every move he makes? Employees need to have proof from their boss that they will be given a fair chance to show what they are capable of doing.

To rebuild workers' self-confidence, you often have to demonstrate your faith in your employees by praising them for previous work or pointing to their knowledge or skills. Employees need to know that you chose them to do a task because of their competence—and, most important, because you trust them to do the job well.

In delegating any assignment, you consider the nature of the task and the ability of the employee. These same issues need to be addressed when you empower your employees.

Fad Solutions

Of the many fads popular today, empowerment may be the biggest. Companies are backing the word with changes in responsibilities and structure. The problem is that these companies and the managers within them expect to see an immediate change.

Instant Empowerment

Rich, a division manager I know, recently complained to me about the situation at his company.

"We've empowered our employees, restructuring to allow them more freedom to get involved in decisions," he told me over drinks, "but nothing has happened. Where are all the great ideas these pundits of empowerment promised?"

I had to remind Rich that his program is less than a year old. Some companies don't see the real results of empowerment until three years have passed. "Even so," he said, "you would expect that one or two employees would come to me with a product idea or some way to save money. Before we restructured, all I heard was that they wanted to contribute to planning, that they wanted to be involved in decisions, that they wanted to help us run the business. Well, now they can. But now I hear nothing from these same employees."

Rich is like a lot of managers who don't realize what a major cultural transformation empowerment is. It's not something you do on Monday, and by Tuesday you are knee-deep in great ideas from employees that will increase market share or immediately grow the bottom line.

No way, particularly in this climate of downsizings. Not only do employees have to be convinced that you are serious about giving them a voice in decisions, but you have to overcome the job insecurities of today's work climate. Given the continuing trend in downsizings, many employees aren't sure whether they can count on a next paycheck. They suffer from a feeling of powerlessness about the future—which is unlikely to stimulate their creativity or their willingness to take risks, which sometimes come with being empowered. So you are likely to receive fewer creative contributions from your employees than you would if job conditions were more favorable.

Look, Boss—No Net

Besides today's volatile business climate, there's another reason your employees will feel frightened by empowerment. Until now, they've operated with a safety net—a boss who answered their questions and made most of the decisions for them. The more you empower your employees, the more you're removing yourself from the picture and eliminating that safety net. And some employees aren't comfortable without it.

For empowerment to be more than a buzzword in your organization, your employees will need to be reassured that (1) you truly intend to empower them, and (2) you will be understanding if they make mistakes. Until you satisfy both of these conditions, employees will be so disenchanted with the idea of empowerment that they are more likely to take those ideas you want from them, put them in a drawer, and store them up for the next company they work for. Hypocrisy has never been easily tolerated by workers, but today's leaner organizations have left employees even less tolerant of management ruses designed to get more work out of them.

Are You Ready for Commitment?

To measure your own commitment to empowerment, ask yourself these questions:

- Are you as excited in others' ideas as your own?
- Do your employees feel free to come to you with their ideas for new products or saving operating expenses, or improving customer service?

- Are procedures cast in concrete or can they be changed if circumstances warrant?
- Are employees recognized for taking risks even when their efforts fail?
- Are mistakes truly seen as training opportunities?
- Do you believe in the ability of your employees to be successful at what they attempt?
- Do you look for reasons to say yes to your employees' ideas before you think of reasons to say no?
- Over the last year, have your staff members taken over any of your former responsibilities?
- Do you have some ways to recognize empowered employees beyond the 4 percent merit increase?
- Do you give employees feedback and encourage them throughout the learning process?
- Do you share not only information on new developments but review organizational basics like values, goals, vision, and the organization's financial situation?

Rethink your management style if you have any "no" answers.

You disempower when you criticize employees' ideas without consideration, talk but don't listen, second-guess employee actions and decisions, give employees tasks with very specific instructions on how the work will be done, constantly hover over your employees, or do everything yourself.

Empowering without preparation—that is, removing the safety net without first preparing your employees—is like letting a young child cross the street alone without first explaining the difference between red and green lights. Employees are very likely to get into trouble if it hasn't been made clear to them what they should and shouldn't do. They'll fall flat on their face, which will discourage them from trying again—and which will discourage you from letting them try, despite all the benefits you could be gaining if you showed a little patience.

Small successes build self-confidence and lead to greater successes. Peers see one of their own succeed and are willing to take on a new assignment, too. But before these other persons take on greater decision-making authority, they will also need grounding in the needed skills. You're making a cultural change in the workplace, and, consequently, it is better to proceed cautiously.

Self-Managed Work Teams

Since some employees may feel safer working within a team structure, you may want to sponsor self-managed work teams (SMWTs) to work on a major task rather than assign the project to a single employee.

SMWTs are empowered groups that work together to accomplish a single task or multiple tasks without the presence of a supervisor or manager. The teams are made up of employees from the same or different levels or areas of the organization and either come together on their own to address a situation or are brought together by a manager who acts as the team's coach but from a distance, maybe attending one or two meetings but saying very little. The manager's role in these SMWTs is to help the team achieve its mission by making accessible to team members needed resources, including access to the manager's own network of contacts who can provide critical resources for the team.

There is a lot of disagreement about whether groups of employees can work together without a formal leader. I think they can be effective, but I also don't believe that SMWTs operate without a leader. SMWTs have leaders, but these leaders change as the group evolves. Likewise, leadership changes as the group moves from one aspect of the subject it is investigating to another. On the basis of members' knowledge, one or another member becomes temporary leader of the group. Depending on when you visit a SMWT as well as on its mission, you might think on one occasion that it is the HR person who is in charge, on another occasion that it is the representative from manufacturing, and on still another occasion that it is the person from engineering. The point is that all these individuals are equals. There is no one in the group who uses positional power to tell the group what it is to do.

In my opinion, that is what makes a group a self-managed work team.

Are these teams better at getting a project completed than a more traditional team led throughout a project by someone in authority? No. Team results depend on the interpersonal, decision-making, and other skills of the team members. Assuming that you have two teams—one SMWT and one led by someone with positional power—and both are equally trained in team management skills, a SMWT will be more productive for you, though. Why? If the team can accomplish its goal or mission with minimum involvement of your time, you use the time savings to focus on other critical issues. In addition, the team members develop or improve important interpersonal and other skills that will help in other projects.

Last week I was at a restaurant having breakfast. Seated next to me at the counter was a woman eating a cheese omelette. "This is the best omelette I've ever tasted," she told me. I looked at my plate. It was good but not great. "Why is this omelette the best you've ever tasted?" I asked her.

"Because I didn't have to make it," she answered, smiling.

That's why SMWTs, if they are successful, are better than leader-led teams. You don't have to lead the group or commit time or energy to the effort; your employees do it all for you. And they come away from the experience motivated and enthusiastic. What more could you ask for?

The Balancing Act

Clearly our earlier experiences with delegation and then with efforts at employee involvement should suggest some ways to make empowerment work—and to reap its benefits.

Your experiences in delegation should teach you about the importance of:

• *Investing in people's knowledge, skills, and ability.* Failure to train is shortsighted, whether your goal is to delegate or empower. When you delegate, you want to be sure that those to whom you delegate a task are capable of handling the responsibility.

In the case of empowerment, training not only can enable

employees to handle the work but can contribute to increased self-esteem, which will make them more comfortable about assuming the greater responsibility that comes with empowerment.

A tip: Besides outside training, you may want to give your employees the opportunity to train each other, thereby adding to your employees' coaching skills.

Training should cover not only skills, abilities, and knowledge for purposes of empowerment but corporate values and business finance. The training in financial management shouldn't be so complex that it is best suited for an economist. I know of one company that built its financial management training around the idea of a children's lemonade stand, which was easily understood by the plant's managers. The company found a way to put complex ideas into simple words and graphs and pie charts, and you can do the same to communicate the key issues facing your operation. Most important, your employees need to know which financial targets are being attained and which ones are being missed. Without this information, your employees won't know where to direct their energies to help the organization prosper.

- *Believing in your employees' abilities to be successful.* You have to trust your employees to do a job well when you delegate—and when you empower. You have to show you have faith in your workers' abilities to make the right decisions.

- *Being clear about your expectations.* When you delegated, you made clear the results you expected. When you empower, you want to be sure that your employees know how you define quality or customer service or the other values you promote within your organization.

- *Building on employees' strengths.* Instead of looking for those occasions when your employees make a mistake, you look for those occasions when they do things right. You don't focus on their weaknesses unless they interfere with either department or team goals. In that case, you create an action plan to remedy the deficiency.

This guideline is as applicable to delegation as it is to empowerment.

- *Sharing information.* If you delegate some task to someone but don't give him or her the latest information to help with that task, it's likely that the person to whom you delegated the work will fail. Those who empower need not only information about new developments but a clear idea of the big picture if they are to make the right decisions. "They don't really care about the organization's goals or objectives," you say. If you're right, then the blame rests with you. A caring attitude is something you as a manager need to be creating in your employees.

• *Putting peer pressure to work.* Go public about accomplishments—sales, profits, deadlines, what have you—to engage employee commitment to improve further in these areas. Recognition helps ensure that delegated work gets done, and it can ensure that employees fully utilize the opportunity to be empowered. Let employees' peers know when their colleagues have broken sales records or identified new product offerings or found ways to reduce accident levels.

As you move toward empowerment, there's one critical bit of advice: *Mean it.* Don't use the word unless you truly are willing to support the effort through thick and thin—which means through moments of great accomplishment and great mistakes. Otherwise, you will wind up with some disappointed, demoralized employees.

Beyond these points, be sure to:

• *Explain your intention.* If employees have become cynical about past promises to involve them in decision making, now is the time to prove you're sincere. You'll have to develop your own campaign to demonstrate by word and deed that you mean it when you say you want employees to make decisions for themselves.

• *Learn not to control others.* You have to demonstrate to your employees by your actions that empowerment isn't just the latest management fad. You mean it when you say that you are willing to share your power. So the next time a situation arises, rather than tell an employee what to do, ask him what should be done. Then ask the employee to do what he has suggested. When your staff member succeeds at the task, offer him praise. Keep this up, allowing the employee to take on more and more difficult tasks on his own. Feelings of self-confidence will develop—and the employee will believe you when you say you are empowering him.

If you think it will help, you might want to meet with each of your staff members to discuss your empowerment plan. At these meetings, you can explain your intention, particularly if in the past you have been more a conventional manager than one who involves employees in decisions.

Ask your employees about their capabilities and if they have thoughts about areas in which they need to improve in order to be fully empowered. Ask them, too, about the types of problems they would like to address or the decisions they would like to handle that they currently aren't. Not only does this demonstrate your desire to empower your employees, it demonstrates your interest in your team's growth and development, something that can't help but motivate your staff to want to be empowered.

• *Move slowly.* Don't get caught up in the hype you find in business publications. Carefully shift decision-making authority to your employees. Continue this process until all those employees who can be empowered are empowered.

• *Keep in mind that not all of your staff members can be empowered.* For those who can't, you may want to find more traditional jobs within your department or organization. If your company as a whole is making this cultural transformation, you may have to consider letting go those employees who no longer fit the new organization's values.

• *Provide guidelines for action.* Your empowered employees need some direction, and you can provide it by reminding them to ask themselves each time they are called upon to make a decision, whether or not the decision they are making is best for the customer and the organization, and reflects the company's goals and values.

There are limits to what empowered employees can do, and they need to know these. Areas beyond employees' purview include modifying work procedures without getting approval from those responsible for initially setting these procedures, hiring or firing workers, and allocating salary increases. These should be self-evident, but you may want to make clear to your employees those areas that remain yours to oversee.

• *Thoroughly explain policies to staff.* It's a good idea to hold periodic meetings to review policies and to ask for ideas to improve them.

• *Don't penalize employees for exceeding their authority to take care of customers' needs.* Let your workers know that you'll support them in dealings with problem customers or customers with unique situations. This will help build their confidence in their interactions with customers.

At the same time:

• *Keep in mind that there is a limit to the mistakes an employee can make.* You want to create a safety net for employees, but at some point you have to step back and ask yourself whether someone is capable of being empowered even with all the training you have provided. Review the operational guidelines once more, and give the person one last chance. Not everyone has the aptitude to be empowered, as well as the willingness.

• *Be patient about results.* One company empowered its workforce because it felt that the change would lead to new product opportunities and operating savings. When there was no significant change in the bottom line six months later, senior management began to complain loudly to their middle managers, who in turn took out the complaints on the employees. No wonder employee morale immediately thereafter dropped.

It took a corporate staff meeting to clear the air.

• *Assign bigger projects to your empowered workers.* Don't limit them anymore to day-to-day assignments. You want them to develop project management skills, which includes determining their own outcomes, deciding what steps to take to achieve the outcomes, choosing the sequence of those steps, and even determining the final deadline.

• *Make sure members of a SMWT know how to proceed.* On the first day, they must begin defining their mission and setting ground rules and, later, clarifying assignments. Depending on the nature of the assigment, the members also need grounding in the problem they are addressing.

Here are some to-dos for you as a team sponsor:

• *Define the task to be done by the team in terms that make its objective clear, specific, and attainable.*

• *Make certain the team is willing to take on this responsibility.* (This is something that can usually be ascertained within the first few minutes of a meeting with team members before you walk away from the effort.)

• *Clarify for the team how achieving its objective fits into the bigger corporate picture.*

• *Become aware of the level of skill needed to complete the task, and determine whether that level is represented by members of the team.* (If not, your options are either to train the team as a whole in these needed skills or to add to the team new members who already possess these skills.)

• *Identify the authority that the team should have and communicate that to the membership.* Decide whether the team is to investigate the problem and report to you on its findings or whether it is to go further and identify alternative solutions and the pros and cons of each and submit this information to you. Maybe you want it to go even further and make its own recommendations and present these or to tell you what it intends to do and then hold off doing it until it gets your OK. Or, further still, act and then report on that action to you.

• *Identify what resources the team will need and arrange for these to be available (dollars, time, equipment).*

• *Identify situations that the team needs to avoid or policies that it needs to abide by.* Communicate these to the members.

• *Clarify the scope of the team's responsibility so that the members know how far they can go both within—up and sideways—and outside the organization to complete their project.*

• *Know what factors will be used to measure the results of the team's effort.*

• *Agree with the team on the type and frequency of communication needed to keep you abreast of team decisions and developments.*

• *Explain to others why this team was formed.* There will be individuals in your organization who may wonder why they weren't chosen for this SMWT. You need to explain your considerations in selecting members for this group and, if you can, promise future team participation for those members of your staff who are not members of this group.

• *Be there when the team needs you.* As sponsor of a SMWT, your role is to be available when the team needs you. That may entail attending a session or two. Your attendance is more to demonstrate your continued interest in the team's efforts than to move the group in any direction.

• *Allow self-scheduling.* Let your employees prioritize their work themselves as well as set deadlines for these assignments. With experience, they will make the right decisions about which assignments to do first, which work to do second, and so on, and finish each by its due date.

If you are reluctant to give your employees this freedom at first, either as individuals or as members of a team, do it progressively. First have them submit to you their to-do list prioritized by A (most important task), B (next in importance), C, and so on. Later, as they develop confidence in their self-scheduling ability and you develop confidence in them, you can sit back and wait for the finished assignment to be done.

• *Encourage risk taking.* Support team efforts to question outmoded ways of getting the work done, even sacred-cow operations whose continuation is eating up revenue.

• *Identify and change those conditions that make employees feel powerless.* Look particularly at bureaucratic rules that impede change initiatives to see if these rules and procedures are really needed or if they are left over from times when employees were told what to do, when to do it, and how to do it.

• *At team sessions, learn to listen, listen, listen.* Make it clear to the team's members that you are there to listen and offer support, not to direct the group. Use the 80/20 rule: Listen 80 percent of the time, and talk about 20 percent or less.

• *Support, support, support.* Don't be afraid to take the heat if your SMWT steps on some toes in its efforts to implement a plan or complete a project. Be there for the team, running interference if need be. Be willing to take some hits in return for the positive reinforcement of team spirit the effort will build.

3

How to Kickstart a Burnt-Out Department

Today's leaner organizations are very stressful places for your employees. Staff who left work at 5 P.M. before now stay regularly until seven. Job and time pressures are bad enough when you need employees with ideas and the energy to implement them. But these stresses are compounded by the feelings of powerlessness that derive from the lack of alternatives to putting up with the situation—the job market offers no alternatives.

No wonder so many employees feel burnt out.

The Problem

Stress over time creates burnout. In a survey of 3,300 employees done by Towers Perrin in 1995, a quarter of the respondents admitted to having difficulty handling the job pressures they are under. Consider the impact on your newly restructured workplace of having a quarter of your staff at risk for burnout or other stress-induced conditions.

The symptoms of burnout take physical and mental forms. It is believed that stress over long periods can cause or aggravate stomach disorders, headaches and backaches, and high blood pressure. It can also cause its victims to be indecisive, indifferent, anxious, and irritable with others.

Those suffering from burnout find it hard to concentrate;

their work is often overdue and/or full of careless mistakes. Studies have also shown that employees who are burnt out and demotivated exhibit less creativity. It's ironic that, although your organization may have restructured in part to benefit from your employees' creativity, many of your employees may be so overtired that they are not equal to the role you're asking them to perform—unless you find a way to reinvigorate and remotivate them.

That's your challenge, and your success as a manager depends on your meeting it. So does your organization's contribution to the bottom line. No one is immune from burnout—not even you. That's why you have to cope with any feelings of demotivation you have before you will be able to cope with your employees' problems. But cope you must. Otherwise, the work of your employees will quickly deteriorate. Your superstars won't shine as brightly. And the ranks of your marginal employees may swell.

WIIFM

Unless you do something about the situation, you could find yourself spending valuable hours counseling overstressed employees with performance problems, maybe even documenting the need for termination of those whom the counseling fails to help. And if your company is in a hiring freeze, you won't be able to replace these individuals. You'll be left with vacancies that won't be filled and work that has to be redistributed to the remaining team members. Which will only—can you guess?—increase their stress level yet again.

The Team Idea

Significantly reducing your employees' workload isn't the solution—even if you could do it, which I doubt. You might be able to ease job pressures by hiring temps and contracting with outside personnel to lend a hand. But that wouldn't eliminate the other stressors—or distressors—that are also factors in employee burnout.

To see the impact of stress factors on a team, look at how they kept one group from using its initiative to help its company.

Led by Bob, the team was made up of members of production, warehousing, shipping, and loading. Despite the opportunity for greater involvement in decisions, the team's members were still angry about the downsizing that had preceded the restructuring. The plant's management had always boasted that it considered its workers family and would never downsize. So the decision to lay off workers came as a shock. The downsizing, followed first by restructuring and then by increased job and time pressures, has made the workers into psychological pressure cookers.

Bob felt that his team needed some evidence that there was a positive side to the restructuring. So he was delighted when Dick from warehousing came up with a way to improve customer service by reducing the time from incoming orders to shipping. The warehouse would be reorganized so that the most popular items were preboxed and all popular items were more accessible. If the project was a success, it would demonstrate to the disbelievers in the team concept—and to those who complained about the amount of time spent in team meetings—that the new organization could give them a bigger say in the functioning of the plant.

Bob wanted to pursue the idea, but the team vetoed it. The members contended that they wouldn't have the time to devote to such a major endeavor.

Job and time pressures were certainly a factor in the team's rejection of the idea, but they weren't the entire reason. Here are the other distressors that Bob's team is experiencing:

• *Lack of clear structure.* The old chain of command in Bob's company, like those in other organizations that have undergone a major organization shift, no longer exists. The pyramidal structure is gone, and most of the walls between departments are gone, too. Reporting relationships are new, and employees have had to find their own way, which has led to frustration when the direction taken has proved to be wrong. Valuable time is being wasted as employees ask for help first from one person and then from another until they find the right individual.

• *Job uncertainty.* So long as downsizing continues to be a strategy to achieve any of a number of management goals, and not solely a Band-Aid for a falloff in sales, employees have reason to worry about being laid off. That's something that members of Bob's team worry about regularly. Tim has a mortgage he needs to pay, Sallie has a kid in college whose tuition is due, and Sam's mother has just gone into a nursing home. They'd like some guarantee that they won't find themselves on the unemployment line before the end of the year.

Talk about layoffs in other companies in their industry only makes it seem as if the world is out to get them. Each assigned task seems like more work to force them to fail and thereby justify termination.

Bob would like not only to reassure his team that its members won't be terminated but also to promise advancement. But he can do neither. So the team continues to worry. And added to that is their suspicion that communications about the issue are taking place but that they aren't in the loop.

• *Lack of trust.* The employees feel they can't trust management. While they like Bob, he is a member of management. So, the team wonders, is Bob endorsing the warehousing plan because it could be beneficial to the organization, or because it could lead to job eliminations?

• *Infrequent feedback.* Bob's team members aren't getting much direction from either Bob or their department heads. Put yourself in their shoes. You are working long hours to do the best job you can. After all, management has told you hard work is key to the company's survival. But you are being given very little direction.

• *Conflicting demands and instructions.* Bob's team is made up of individuals who now have two bosses—Bob, their team's leader, and their department head. Only a few months into the reorganization, two of the teams members have already found themselves involved in work for the team that conflicts with the efforts of their department supervisor. And team assignments often have the same priority as assignments from their department head. Under those circumstances, team members are reluctant to take on a project that could take significant time away from their regular work.

• *A feeling of powerlessness.* Despite the restructuring, there are still pockets of traditional management within the organization, and the warehousing idea will require the support of the people who head up these areas. Because several of these areas have been risk-averse in the past, the team doubts it could get their support this time.

They're no more inclined to take a major risk, either. With no opportunities for jobs elsewhere in the industry, they don't want to chance failure and consequently the loss of their jobs. They don't believe Bob when he tells them that management will view mistakes as learning experiences.

• *Role ambiguity.* Role ambiguity occurs when responsibility to do something within the team isn't well defined.

At Bob's company, it still isn't clear what it means to be a team member. What is Bob's responsibility? How are teams to interact? Who will be responsible for what? Responsibilities seem as clear as mud.

• *Lack of resources to get the work done.* At Bob's company, team members have heard a lot of promises for equipment, additional workers, and so on, then had these deferred until the next budget round because the industry in which the company operates is still in a downturn.

In addition to to the distressors experienced by Bob's team, other factors can come into play in other situations:

• *Changing roles.* Think about it. One day, you're in charge, and the next you're a coach or a facilitator. Or, in the case of employees, having been an independent worker, you suddenly become part of a team with responsibility not only for individual tasks but for the growth of the business.

• *Unclear expectations.* No one is certain what to expect in today's horizontal organizations—neither former supervisors who now find themselves coaching teams nor employees who make up those teams.

- *Bureaucracy.* Even in our restructured organizations, bureaucracies still exist. Too many companies have created new structures—teams—to generate ideas while retaining the bureaucracies that require the signatures of 100 people to get the ideas implemented.

- *Unrealistic expectations.* Today's employees are already stretched beyond their limits; being asked to do the impossible only adds to the pressures they are experiencing from trying to do the possible.

- *Loss of critical talent.* In today's lean organizations, key positions may remain vacant, or the work may be handled either by someone unqualified to do it or by someone who has the skills to perform the task but who has little time to do it right.

- *The fear of failure.* Stress comes from fear of being unable to do the work that's critical to the department's bottom line. Political gamesmanship, and cronyism are more important than competence and capability.

- *Overload.* Crises come one after another. And there are fewer staff members today to firefight.

- *Reversal of decisions.* Frustration grows as management shifts vital resources from one goal to another, and in the end nothing at all gets accomplished.

To determine if your employees are victims of job and time pressures and other distressors, ask yourself these questions about your staff members:

- Are they continuously irritable or angry at work?
- Do they complain regularly about their workloads?
- Do they have to rush from one task to another?
- Do you find them regularly eating lunch at their desks or staying late to complete work assignments?
- Do they worry about their job and talk about the impact of downsizing on their own personal situations?
- Do they complain about their inability to stay abreast of developments in their fields?
- Do they complain that they have no say in decisions being made?
- Do they see no rewards for the effort they are putting in?

If the answer is yes to some or all of these questions, then burnout may be a problem. (Incidentally, ask yourself these questions as well; remember, you're not immune from the condition.)

Back to the Basics

In the past, burnout was addressed through job enrichment and job redesign, adding new elements to existing jobs to give employees the opportunity to gain individual recognition and increase their sense of self-worth. The idea was to make the job more meaningful by enriching it through the incorporation of new tasks.

Managers were also encouraged to make employees feel more involved in the work by relating the tasks they did to the final product or service sold by the company. A motivating job was one that included all those tasks needed to complete a product or handle a customer. An engineer might be responsible for the complete design of a product, or a customer service rep might be given all the correspondence having to do with an account.

Frequent feedback was critical. The thinking was that employees' interest in their work could be increased if they had a clear idea whether they hit the mark or not. Even if it was the latter, the knowledge would encourage them to try again—provided they were motivated by challenges. In other words, people had different needs. All that a manager could do was create a work environment that would satisfy the needs of as many people as possible. But managers were alerted that there would be some people who just could not be motivated.

The move to enrich and redesign jobs to incorporate factors that would increase job satisfaction came from the work of motivational theorists like Abraham Maslow, Frederick Herzberg, David C. McClelland, and George Elton Mayo, who identified factors that contributed to job satisfaction and dissatisfaction. Managers were encouraged to learn more about their employees so that they could apply the right motivators to the right employees. In short, different strokes for different folks.

Maslow hypothesized a pyramidal hierarchy of needs. At the lowest level are physiological needs—needs for food, drink, and shelter. The next level of need is safety, which included needs for security, stability, and freedom from fear. The third level of needs—social needs—involves friendships and contacts with others. Esteem and self-actualization are at the highest level of the pyramid. Esteem needs are met when we feel important or are needed by others, and self-actualization needs are fulfilled when we realize our full potential. At the time that Maslow reported his findings, 85 percent of those he surveyed were satisfied in their physiological needs, 70 percent in their safety needs, 50 percent in their social needs, 40 percent in their ego needs, and only 10 percent in their self-actualizing needs. So, Maslow contended, little would come from corporate efforts to make jobs safer or to provide higher pay. The big payoff in terms of performance would come, he believed, from giving employees the opportunity to realize more of their potential on the job.

To some extent, Herzberg's conclusions, as described in his Two-Factor Theory, were similar. Herzberg divided people's needs into five dissatisfiers and five satisfiers. The five satisfiers included achievement, recognition, interesting responsibilities, positive work relationships, and opportunity for growth. The five dissatisfiers were supervision (a manager willing to teach and delegate responsibility), administration (including good communication with the worker), working conditions, interrelationships, and salary (adequate compensation). He went on to suggest that a good hygienic environment, the latter, could prevent job dissatisfaction but couldn't affect satisfaction. Only the job satisfiers could do that.

McClelland identified the needs of self-motivated achievers, who he believed made up about 10 percent of the population. These achievers preferred to set their own goals, set goals that were tough but realistic, and preferred tasks that provided them with immediate feedback. He felt it was possible to build achievement traits into jobs by including personal responsibility, individual participation in setting productivity targets, creation of moderate goals, and fast, clear-cut feedback on results.

Finally, Mayo argued in favor of small work groups in motivating workers. He felt that when people become part of an informal work group, they experience a social relationship that increases their performance. His research was supported by the experiences of Japanese companies in using teams. And early experiences of U.S. companies with teams in the late 1980s and early 1990s prompted our current love affair with teams.

Fad Solutions

Today, teamwork and empowerment have become seductive solutions to the problem of burnout. Convenience benefits and monetary rewards have also entered the picture.

The Magic of Teamwork

Managements see teams as a powerful cure-all for the post-downsizing and restructuring emotions that could poison productivity and profitability. As a consequence, you could say that U.S. companies are teaming up with teams. After most downsizings, there seems to be an awful lot of talk about the concept of teamwork, about the value of everyone pulling together, and about how collaboration will enable an ailing organization to get through an economic downturn.

No question, Mayo was correct: In many instances more can be done by several people working together than by one individual working alone. But not every situation requires teamwork, as corporate experience with teams seems to suggest. The results range from outstanding to mediocre, depending on factors both within and outside the team. Certainly, teamwork is not a panacea. When it comes to burnout, sometimes working within a group can make the work easier and more fun and overcome workers' fears and concerns, and sometimes it can make a meeting a bloody hell. After all, not everyone can work well together. And time is precious. Meetings that accomplish very little, no matter the good intentions of the team leader, are not motivational.

Bill, a manager I know, has clearly found that out.

His company downsized, and he found himself responsible

for the work of four additional employees; their supervisor had been laid off. Bill was told, "They'll have adjustment problems, but team meetings should overcome them. Make the employees think like a team."

The idea of holding regular weekly meetings made sense, since communication generally brings people together. But Bill's team meetings serve solely as a forum for the exchange of information. Despite the availability of other communication mediums (like e-mail), Bill holds operational meetings twice a week—for a total of three hours. He and his staff meet once at the start of the week to plan activities and once at the end of the week to evaluate results. The time is spent talking about new policies and group mores; not much time is spent doing any real work.

Three hours in meetings seems a lot of time for a downsized department, but that's not the end of it, not at all. Besides the two operational meetings, Bill and his staff are involved in several cross-functional groups that meet regularly.

Bill recently told me that he and his staff feel burnt out—and I believe with cause. Since the downsizing, Bill and his expanded staff have picked up more work, work long hours to get their new work done, and spend many valuable hours in useless meetings.

The results are not spectacular, either, which may be due to the fact that the workplace itself is not congenial. Fear management is being practiced by many senior executives who wrongly believe that the threat of further layoffs will prompt greater creativity and productivity from the staff. With no job movement available within the industry and few, if any, promotional opportunities and rewards available within the company, employees feel corralled.

Even the most cooperative of team members can't always surmount these bad external vibes.

The "E" Word

Equally in vogue, empowerment can make routine jobs more exciting, as well as tap into a wellspring of underutilized human capital for the organization. This may explain the management rhetoric about it. But empowerment isn't a guaranteed solution to burnout. Certainly it isn't if the empowered employee has not been trained to handle his new responsibilities, and many organizations that advocate that managers empower their employees do not provide the needed training for either the managers who will be empowering or the employees who will be empowered. Under such circumstances, too often employees who are told they are empowered are soon told they are also incompetent in doing what they were told they were empowered to do.

On the plus side, empowerment can enrich workers' jobs, which can contribute to revitalization. But burnt-out employees too easily become cynical and see empowerment as a tactic to get more work from them.

Convenience Benefits

On a more practical level, today's companies are trying to motivate employees by helping them deal with their time stresses. To do this, they offer on-site personal services called "convenience benefits." The conveniences range from on-site postal services to gift stores, to hairdressers, to concierge services that purchase movie and theater tickets and arrange to have clothing washed and picked up at the laundromat.

With employees putting in nine-hour workdays and two to three hours each weekend, according to a 1995 U.S. Chamber of Commerce study, help in dealing with personal errands does make sense. On-site dry cleaning pickup, for instance, means one less errand between the end of the workday and dinner.

Unfortunately, for employees who are already so burnt out that they can't see the positive side of anything, convenience benefits, like empowerment, are perceived as a trick of management to get them to put in longer hours. If management takes care of your errands for you, you have no excuse to refuse overtime because "I have to pick up tickets for a matinee show my son wants to see."

This attitude toward convenience benefits is a pity because

for some employees—for instance, single parents and dual-career couples—they are a godsend. Still, a survey by the journal *Compensation & Benefits Review* found them valued way below any other corporate benefits.

Monetary Rewards

Any discussion about motivation can't ignore reference to money. Monetary reward is being used today in two ways to motivate.

To align more closely performance and pay, as well as to motivate, companies have set up a number of performance-based incentive programs, covering all levels and responsibilities. Most of the compensation plans add to the base salary for achievement of corporate goals, but there are also plans now that place a portion of employees' base pay at risk by tying it to corporate performance, reducing pay when goals aren't achieved. These plans motivate when times are good and management plans work, but demotivate when either economic downturns or poor senior management decisions negatively impact the bottom line.

In team-based organizations, companies are pilot-testing ways to reward individual and team effort.

Both efforts are based on the same thinking: Money can motivate. They're right: A big bonus can inspire a sudden burst of energy. On the other hand, an increase in performance from a bonus is usually short-lived. Performance declines once the money is spent. There is also the danger that money, when given as a reward for outstanding performance, becomes seen as an entitlement—something that's expected.

One company had two outstanding years. The third year brought a major shift downward in sales. Employees had received relatively large bonuses the first two years; in the third year, they still received bonuses, but only a quarter as large as those they had got during each of the previous two years. Staff was up in arms. Management had to hold a special meeting to address the morale problems that had developed—although, remember, the company, which was beginning to experience economic problems, didn't have to give employees anything.

Still another danger with using money as a motivator: It can replace intrinsic motivators, like the challenge of confronting a problem and solving it or the pleasure of finishing a task on time.

Maybe worse is how money is often linked to performance. Within teams, members talk about how difficult it is to fairly compensate outstanding performers. And while there are some interesting experiments under way as I write this, to date the problem of objective assessment by team members of their peers appears extremely difficult. There is also some doubt in my mind about the ability of outsiders to objectively assess team participants.

The problem with variable pay programs occurs when the goals linked to rewards are not within employees' grasp, adding to employee frustrations. Besides, today's overworked employees feel they already deserve bonuses for taking on the extra work from employees who were laid off without receiving additional pay.

None of this is to suggest that money shouldn't be used as a motivator, only that it should not be used as the sole motivator. It should be used, however. Its lack is clearly a demotivator. Money is a form of recognition; employees use it to measure their achievement, importance to the organization, and standing among others within the organization.

The Balancing Act

Empowerment and team management—two of the buzzwords of the 1990s—are clearly extensions of job enrichment and job redesign. This clearly ties team management, empowerment, and other efforts to increase employee participation to the motivational theories of the early 1960s.

But times have changed dramatically since the Hierarchy of Needs or the Two-Factor Theory were introduced.

Maslow argued that the lower physiological, safety, and social needs had to be satisfied before individuals could focus on meeting their higher level needs. Herzberg contended that dissatisfiers had to be dealt with before motivational factors could stimulate performance. When Maslow and Herzberg published their theories more than forty years ago, this sequencing didn't represent a problem—there were layoffs, but employees could expect soon to be rehired; companies were not going through the transition they are now, so dissatisfiers weren't a major problem, either. But today, due to downsizing and restructuring, the lower needs of Maslow's hierarchy and the hygiene factors in Herzberg's Two-Factor Theory are no longer givens. Just the opposite.

Remember that when Maslow and Herzberg shared their research findings, Maslow reported that U.S. workers were 85 percent satisfied in their physiological needs, 70 percent satisfied in their safety needs, and 50 percent satisfied in their social needs. Today, with downsizings announced almost daily, could we say the same?

It seems that our boundaryless organizations are seeking, through concepts like teams and empowerment, to meet self-actualization needs at the same time that many employees feel that their job security (that is, a safety need) is threatened, and still other employees feel that their contributions are not being recognized (esteem needs). Likewise, if we consider Herzberg's Two-Factor Theory in light of today's restructured organizations, we see broad acceptance of the idea of motivation factors but less consideration given to the dissatisfiers: Job expectations are unclear; workplaces have become literally sweatshops, with employees expected to do too much in too little time; in an effort to give employees freedom to use their initiative, supervisors and managers often don't give them sufficient direction; and there is lots of talk but not much communication.

Even if we discount Maslow's contention that lower-level needs need to be satisfied before loftier issues are of importance to employees, we still have Herzberg's contention that failure to address the dissatisfiers can demotivate employees. Consequently, if we're to get the benefits of allowing our employees to have greater participation in decision making, we have to address these hygiene or maintenance factors. If we are to make our restructured, team-based organizations work successfully, we need to reexamine our own operating styles to see how they can support the basic needs and maintenance factors while also managerially and organizationally responding to people's higher needs and wants. Maybe this involves the application of plain old good supervision.

Freeing Workers to Flourish

Translated into day-to-day actions, motivating employees and allowing them to thrive in the new environment means ensuring that, as they leave their plants or offices each day physically tired, they do not have their minds filled with questions like these:

- Will I be able to keep my job? (Even knowing that the answer is no is better than not knowing at all.)
- How has my organization's expectations of my performance changed? What can I do about it? Training?
- Will my pay be affected? (If it will be, employees want to know so that they can act, not react.)
- Will I be demoted? (So long as there are opportunities to learn the skills to help the employee eventually return to his or her current position, even a yes answer will be appreciated. Better to know than to spend sleepless nights worrying about it.)
- What role will I play in this team? Am I fully contributing?

If you fail to provide answers to questions like these, you open the door to nagging doubts about job security and your expectations. You also contribute to budding cases of employee burnout when you:

- Give your employee an unclear assignment.
- Play favorites.
- Provide unclear or constantly changing work requirements.
- Withhold information so that employees don't have a clear picture of a project or problem.
- Fail to deliver on promises or agreements.

- Fail to support an employee's efforts by providing necessary money, staff, equipment, or other support.
- Nitpick about work performance during a tight time crunch.
- Hog the credit for yourself when you could just as easily share it.
- Demand that too much be done in too short a time.
- Change any job requirements without letting the employee responsible for the work know.
- Grant authority that is not commensurate with the responsibilities you've assigned an employee.
- Give an illogical assignment to someone whose to-do list is two pages long.
- Fail to trust your employees or credit them with intelligence or creativity; demean them.
- Shirk from making decisions that are critical to employees' completion of their work on time.

All of these managerial misbehaviors are tied to the distressors mentioned earlier in this chapter and reflect satisfaction of hygiene needs.

Some Managerial Do's

Besides these don'ts, there are a number of do's that can minimize the feelings of stress your employees are experiencing. The following guidelines recognize the need to satisfy lower-level motivational needs as well as higher ones, hygiene factors as well as motivational ones. They reflect the new partnership between employees and their organizations in which employees are responsible for taking the initiative to develop and enhance skills and are expected to actively seek ways to help sustain and grow the business. Managers' responsibility, in turn, is to:

- *Provide employees the information they need to do a good job.* Just as not including employees in the loop causes stress and ultimately burnout, providing a climate for open communications and clear goal setting gives employees a sense of control that minimizes feelings of stress.

- *Provide regular feedback.* With constant but informal feedback, you can keep your employees from worrying unnecessarily about their job performance. You can also keep them from taking the wrong tack with a particular project and not becoming aware of this until after the project is completed.

In today's workplace, neither you nor your employees can afford to waste time. There isn't time to redo something that could have been done right in the first place had there been proper communication.

- *Learn to say "thank you" regularly.* In doing so, be specific about the behavior you are acknowledging. A general "Thanks for all you've done" will mean nothing compared to a very specific "Thank you for putting in those extra hours yesterday evening to ensure that the potential customer received it in time. It enabled me to prepare a better presentation, so we got the account." Note how this comment not only states exactly how the employee contributed but describes the impact of the employee's actions on your actions and the organization's objective.

- *Involve employees in decisions that affect their jobs.* This was the purpose behind much of the restructuring. Practice makes perfect—and your employees, familiar with the way the work gets done, can come up with solutions that can contribute to your organization's competitive advantage.

And being involved—and truly listened to—will reinvigorate staff and generate enthusiasm for plans.

- *Publicly recognize employees for good work.* A deserved pat on the back can be very motivating. It shows an employee that you're aware of her contribution to the team's objective, particularly if the employee had to work long and hard to make that contribution. Recognition can stimulate the employee to work even harder and accomplish even more.

Incidentally, when you recognize a member of your team, you become a cheerleader for the whole group. Small successes lead to a willingness to attempt bigger projects with larger returns.

If you can't provide bonuses or promotions, then look to other forms of recognition. For instance, if your team is working hard on a difficult project, you could show your support by doing such little things as bringing in doughnuts for the group or asking how an employee's family is coping with the employee's having longer work hours and less time with the kids—in other words, anything that not only demonstrates to the team members that you consider them valuable workers but shows that you realize they are valuable as persons, too.

• *Distribute rewards fairly.* Employees want to be sure that they are as eligible for the rewards as the next person, that is, that there is no favoritism about whose work gets acknowledged and rewarded.

• *Establish easy-to-use channels of communication.* You want to create means by which employees can ask questions and get answers—both a formal means (such as a regular biweekly operational meeting) and an informal means (such as keeping your door open several hours a day as an invitation to staff members to drop by to discuss problems or project progress).

These channels of communication may provide opportunities to vent more than ways to communicate, but learning what troubles your employees isn't so bad, is it? It's still a step in increasing job satisfaction.

• *See that employees get the resources they need to do their work.* They need not only the right equipment (they don't necessarily need the most up-to-date; they need the equipment that is best suited to the work they will be doing) but access to people who can lend a hand.

• *Give employees good work to do.* Make the tasks you delegate challenging. If your employees are growing bored from doing routine work (lots of routine work), you can reinvigorate them by assigning a task that opens up an opportunity to learn something new or break ground in a new corporate direction.

Look at job assignment as a means of increasing employability and promote it as such. While you can't promise job security—who can, in these days of downsizing?—you can provide opportunities to increase an employee's value to your organization or, at worst, to improve his ability to find another job should he lose the current one.

But remember that there is also too much "motivation." If an employee is evidently burnt out and suffering from work overload, look for ways to reduce her responsibilities or provide her with assistance, from the use of temps and interns to delegating work over the short term to others while the employee recoups.

• *Be alert to employee needs for help.* Don't wait until the problem has you considering terminating the employee. Consider referring an employee who is overstressed to your company's employee assistance program (EAP). Counseling won't eliminate the problem, but the employee may learn to cope with the distressors.

If the stressors are related more to department mores or your style than to the weight of the employee's workload, a one-on-one interview with the employee may clear the air.

Dick, head of information systems, would have lost a very talented employee if he hadn't called her into his office to discuss problems she was having with internal customers.

One of the department's best troubleshooters, Amelia saw her performance begin to erode as she encountered one system problem after another following the company's relocation to a new building and setup of a new mainframe. Some of the problems were due to the system changeover, but many more were due to Dick's laid-back style of management, which Amelia felt had brought about the problems. The new technology was incompatible with existing hardware, for example, and Dick had been responsible for approving the new system. Further, none of the company's employees had been trained on the new system, so work on many of the serious system problems was delayed due to calls from users who just did not know how to handle the new e-mail and word-processing systems.

Although angry with Dick, Amelia took it out on coworkers/users, snapping at them, responding condescendingly to their queries, and otherwise adding to the stress everyone was under.

Dick finally intervened when Amelia snapped at the CEO's secretary for her inability to access the correct computer port to print a document. He called her into his office.

To get the conversation going, Dick asked, "How's it going?" But it opened a floodgate of emotions, and Dick was wise enough to listen empathically to what Amelia said. While Dick had to admit that some of her complaints were valid, he also felt she was unaware of some of the issues that the company had to address in selecting the new technology for the relocated headquarters, particularly the tight budgetary constraints. Amelia also wasn't aware of corporate plans to initiate a major training program on the new software as soon as everyone was settled in.

Amelia felt better when she left. Dick realized he hadn't maintained communications as well as he should have with his staff or been as watchful as he should have of the effects of the relocation on their jobs. He promised himself that he would keep his department informed of the why of decisions as well as the decisions themselves.

• *Eliminate petty criticism.* There is always room for improvement, but nitpicking is not constructive. Praise should come first, followed by suggestions for improvement that aren't about petty matters. I know that you are busy, too, but never think that you are too busy to offer praise. Think how you would feel if your own supervisor felt he was too busy to acknowledge your accomplishments.

• *Don't create needless stress for your employees.* We've already listed some of management don'ts. But there are very important supervisory caveats. For instance, don't create arbitrary deadlines or vacillate about a decision, or criticize a team member during a group session, or become abusive when you address a work problem, or pit employees against one another, or deliberately make comments that make employees feel threatened about the loss of their jobs. In other words, don't allow yourself to take your own feelings of stress out on your employees.

• *Recognize behaviors as well as outcomes.* Most award systems recognize outcomes solely. But failure to acknowledge a change in behavior is a lost opportunity to motivate an employee to improve his skills, habits, or process.

This may sound like management basics, and it is. But team management and empowerment need the foundation of these basics for them to work. If you're looking for something new to do, consider some new ways of doing these. For example, why not acknowledge an employee's contribution at a team party? Make it a breakfast occasion, with coffee and danish. And save the work discussion for later. Or "do lunch," again with the provision that no one is to talk work. (For the workaholics in the bunch, that may be a tough session to survive, but it's great for building a sense of camaraderie among team members.)

However you practice these motivational guidelines, the message you want is the same: You care about your employees.

One last reminder: Consider your own state of health and well-being. To determine if you are stressed out, ask yourself:

• Do you feel like a target? If you do, you want to ask yourself why. If it has to do with your relationship with your boss, maybe it's time for a meeting in which you express your feelings. If you are overstressed, consider a stress reduction program.

• Are you bottling up your anger? If the answer is yes, you should learn to be more assertive about those desires and opinions that are important to you. But, remember, be assertive, not aggressive or confrontational.

• Do you think to give yourself little rewards occasionally? Positive rewards not only reinforce behavior but also contribute to stress reduction. How about a movie instead of lunch on a workday?

• Do you believe only in Murphy's Law? Forget that Murphy' Law says that anything that can go wrong will. Instead, develop a more optimistic and positive attitude toward life. Turn off the negative self-talk. Research suggests that your attitude about yourself is your most important asset in coping with stress.

• Do you listen too often, too, to an inner voice that keeps telling you "you should" do this or that? If so, turn it off, too. Learn to pace yourself.

• Do you try to be perfect in everything you do? Give it up. This kind of attitude is not only self-defeating but also a stress producer. Focus, instead, on your strengths. Recognize your worth.

4

A New Relationship: Aloyalty

If there were a marker that could be placed on the front stoops of many of today's leaner organizations, these organizations' downsized employees might want it to say:

Company Loyalty
Died 199X

Is corporate loyalty dead? Yes, if we're talking about employee commitment tied to a tradition of guaranteed employment, with a career ladder for promotion, for those employees who show up on time and give more than a full day's work for a full day's pay.

American employees saw such a commitment as a social contract between them and their organizations, but how realistic were they in believing in it? After all, the name of the corporate game is profitability, and companies have a bottom line to protect. It is inevitable that some companies will have to let people go, even very good people, to do that. Still, people believed in corporate loyalty until the 1980s, because historically, periods of downsizings were followed by periods of rehirings. People might not have been able to find a job at their previous employer, but they could find work at the same level for the same or *more* money at another company. And that's not true anymore.

A research study reported in *The New York Times* found that of those full-time employees who lost jobs in 1991 and 1992, only 35 percent were lucky enough to find full-time employment at comparable pay by January 1994. The other 65 percent were working at lower-paying jobs, working part-time, or still unemployed.

Victims of the corporate ax—whether members of the 35 percent or the 65 percent—are still adjusting to the reality that the American dream of steady career advancement within the security of a corporate family was just that—a dream. So, too, the survivors, who feel no dedication to their companies and have become cynical about their organizations' promises about a better future. Which is why this issue of lost corporate loyalty, whether or not this social contract stood on a firm foundation, is a management issue.

The Problem

Given a glutted job market that offers no alternatives to their current positions, most employees don't want to risk losing their current jobs, so they do the work they're given, taking advantage of any learning opportunities that come their way. "I can't take any chances because getting my next job may depend on what I learn in this one," one employee told me. Her plant had recently upgraded its manufacturing process. But this employee and others—survivors of downsizings—still harbor ill feelings toward the organization that laid off their former peers. And they show their feelings in their attitudes about customer service or TQM or other corporate initiatives designed to increase competitive advantage, in their relationships with their supervisors, and in their response to upper-management communications and corporate policies in general. Some look for malicious but subtle ways to even the score, like not processing that customer order as quickly as their boss promised or commiting acts of pilferage. While there's no evidence to show that the rise in employee theft across corporate America is tied to downsizings, many experts see a relationship between loss of employee loyalty and loss of supplies from petty thefts.

Job résumés are up to date. If employees hear of an opportunity elsewhere, they pursue it more quickly than they might have done a few years ago. And if they get the job, they are gone in a shot, without giving the usual two weeks. After all, why shouldn't they? They're putting in 110 percent on the job—maybe are being praised to the skies by you—but they could find themselves on the unemployment line as quickly as a layabout who can't be counted on. To appreciate how survivors of downsizings might feel, consider this real situation at one plant reported by a colleague of mine.

The company had let people go in groups. Management held a meeting with each group about severance benefits, whereupon the group's members were led out of the building by security guards—in full view of dozens of current workers who couldn't help but wonder about whether they awaited a similar fate. My colleague wryly titled the story, "Now We Know How Thanksgiving Turkeys Must Feel."

We can appreciate on a more personal basis how individuals feel who were displaced but now have jobs by looking at what happened to Rick.

A Case Study in Changing Times

Rick was a programmer for a major technology company. He had had nothing but outstanding appraisals. Thanks to his efforts in creating a new line of software products and games for a newly acquired division, the division's revenues had grown from $35 million to $100 million. But the division's profit margin wasn't enough to satisfy the board. The company sold the division, and Rick, at age 54 with more than twenty-three years with the corporation, was let go. It was one of several downsizings that the company had undertaken. The layoff came as a shock to Rick; but even more upsetting was the response to his résumé from corporate recruiters.

Rick learned that loyal service to a company meant nothing in the job market. In fact, it worked against him. Those executives with whom he met felt he "lacked initiative," although he could point to many times he had played key roles in developing and expanding new businesses for his former company.

In years past, job hopping was frowned upon. But now those who move from job to job are credited for their flexibility and adaptability. Companies that had reputations for never letting employees go during a downturn now look down on employees who have worked more than a decade with the same organization; they see the time these workers spent at one company as confirmation of professional mediocrity.

Rick now has a full-time job, but he is also developing a software package on his own that he hopes to market. And though he's relatively new at his current company, his résumé is available to any company that requests it. His loyalty is to only one person—himself. He'll job-hop from now on if it ensures him a stable career. Multiply that situation by ten, twenty, or thirty employees, and consider what a company loses when employees no longer feel any commitment to the organization.

Along with employee loyalty, companies are losing other benefits:

- *Lower hiring costs (e.g., recruiting fees, interviewing costs, and relocation expenses).* For some industries, the savings are greater than others; the insurance industry, for one, generally has to hire three entry-level employees to get one long-term employee.

- *Training costs.* New hires may need some classroom training as well as on-the-job learning. Should the employees stay, the training becomes an investment. Should they leave, the funds and time that were spent were wasted.

- *Productivity.* People who remain for some time with a company can perform their jobs more efficiently and with less supervision than those who have spent less time with the company. If they enjoy their jobs and have good work relationships with their managers, they also are more motivated and work harder.

- *Employee referrals.* Long-term employees recommend only high-calibre candidates to their company, which raises the level of skill of new hires and also cuts recruiting costs, because the company doesn't have to go to an outside search firm for job candidates.

- *High-quality products and customer service.* Those who do

their jobs well from long experience with the organization produce quality products, appreciate the need for good customer
relationships, and go the extra mile to ensure customer reten-
tion.

WIIFM

"Why should this problem concern me?" you ask. "Granted,
there are costs to the company, but so long as there are still Ricks
out there looking for jobs, I needn't worry. If I lose a talented
worker to another company, there are others I can hire. I don't
have to worry either about having troublemakers or those with
bad attitudes. They, too, can be replaced."

Maybe, but addressing attitudinal problems can take up a
lot of your management time. If you've ever had to fire someone
for such a reason, you know the amount of time you'll need to
spend in counseling and then documenting that counseling to
justify the termination in a court of law. Better to stop the likelihood of attitudinal problems in the first place by acknowledging
your employees' insecurities about their jobs and reaffirming
their value to the organization. One of the worst things you as a
manager can do is to deny the situation and pretend that your
employees have no reason to be frightened or insecure about
their futures.

When employees leave your organization to go to other
jobs, it's also likely that you'll be losing your best performers,
the ones you'll need to run effectively your leaner organization;
after all, they'll be the ones other companies will want, too. At a
critical time in your company's history, you'll be losing skills,
abilities, and knowledge that are important to your department's mission and the continuity of your organization.

What can you do to build commitment to your organization, the loyalty of the 1990s? Clearly you should *not* do the following:

• Flaunt your special privileges as a member of management, like an expense account with which you can take friends
to lunch if you want.

- Tell employees that they can be easily replaced and by those who will work for smaller paychecks.

- Confine the use of training efforts to situations in which the company will directly and immediately benefit.

- Be deaf to employees' suggestions; if that doesn't discourage them, remind your staff members to hang on to their ideas in case they ever make it to management.

- Keep information about company projects, deals, and new policies a secret from employees.

- Show little interest in employees' personal lives, or tell them that they should keep their personal problems at home where they belong.

Back to the Basics

Ten or twenty years ago, you could assure survivors of a downsizing that their colleagues would soon be back once the economic downswing was over. If someone was downsized, you could recommend several nearby companies at which she could apply for a comparable job until your organization's financial situation improved and it began to hire again.

The beginnings of outplacement counseling in the 1970s were evident, but these early firms provided help mainly with writing résumés and preparing the laid-off for job interviews or decisions about the need to relocate to stay in the same field at the same pay.

If you could, you stayed in the same company. It made sense for an employee to devote thirty to forty years to an organization where the company had career tracks that ensured advancement for those who put in that 110 percent effort.

Fast Tracks

Entry-level employees whose school backgrounds suggested that they had the technical or administrative skills that the organization needed would find themselves on fast tracks that were designed to prepare them for key positions within twelve months or sooner. I myself was in such an internship program early in my publishing career, part of a program designed to give liberal arts graduates the business skills it was felt we would need to succeed in the business world.

Assessment centers existed. Companies sent those employees they judged to have high potential to gain better insights into the skills they had and the skills they needed to develop to move up within the organization. There were career paths for managers and career paths for nonmanagers, even two-tier career paths for technicians so that they could choose whether to stay within their technical field or move into management. Coaching and counseling of these fast-trackers was ongoing.

Training was designed to help employees not only with their current jobs but also with the jobs that management expected they would eventually assume.

Some companies had succession programs that identified potential successors for every key position within the organization, monitored these individuals' evaluations twice a year, identified training programs that could help them overcome skill deficiencies, and updated the succession plans annually on the basis of performance evaluations. Even those who weren't on these career paths could look forward to a relatively secure career with the same organization and the retirement party with the promised gold watch.

Whether true or not, there was a sense of family associated with the job—a relationship built on a belief that the organization cared for your well-being.

Fad Solutions

In the late 1990s, management seems to be trying to reestablish corporate loyalty that has been lost in wave after wave of downsizing.

Outplacement is a critical part of the formula, not only to help those downsized but to communicate to the survivors that the company wants to treat its employees fairly. There are counselors whose job it is to teach managers how to handle layoffs in a sensitive manner, including how to tell the employee he is being let go, how to communicate to the rest of the staff the action taken, and how to handle any long-term impact on survivors, such as feelings of guilt.

When a colleague is terminated, employees usually have mixed emotions about the situation. They are saddened and feel sympathetic toward their former colleague, but they also cannot help feeling some relief that they were not the one chosen to leave. Managers and supervisors are being taught how to talk to their staff and discuss how the employee will be missed and how to present a plan of how the staff will absorb the extra workload.

Companies have come to recognize, however, that these sessions with employees aren't enough to restore commitment or a sense of goodwill toward management. Consequently, more and more organizations are instituting a three-step process to reestablish the loyalty and commitment they may have lost from the downsizing, according to research conducted by Hay Associates. The plan calls for: (1) establishing a partnership relationship with employees through greater employee participation; (2) developing compensation and benefits programs that consider both the financial and the family needs of the employee and family-related perks; and (3) providing opportunities for personal and professional development.

Let's look at these three elements more closely.

1. *The partnership relationship.* The new relationship is based on greater employee involvement in the creation of the organization's mission and strategic and operational plans. It involves participative management or participative management taken one step further, to empowerment. The thinking is that the sharing of this management responsibility with employees will lead to greater employee commitment to the goals of the organization.

Critical to this new relationship is making information about the business accessible to employees. Company newsletters, full staff meetings, and e-mail are just some means that companies can use to provide the knowledge employees need to positively influence results.

2. *Compensation and benefits programs.* The compensation side includes variable pay plans that provide bonuses and other incentive opportunities that previously weren't available to those in certain positions, such as warehouse workers or secretaries. The idea is to generate interest and excitement by giving employees a financial stake in the business.

The benefits side is made up of offering work at home, flexible schedules, work sharing, and cafeteria benefits. The idea is that the person most familiar with family needs should make the decisions about the benefits he will receive. Management's message is this: We care about you as an individual; in turn, we would like you to care about your company. It's a sales campaign in which an attractive financial/benefits package is being offered in return for commitment by employees to the company's mission and goals.

3. *Professional and personal development.* The buzzword is "employability." Companies admit that they can't guarantee employees lifetime employment, but they can help their employees develop the skills they'll need to find another job if, because of corporate circumstances, they have to be laid off. The idea is to give employees portable skills, abilities, and knowledge—to replace job security with career security.

Employability is achieved by providing training in areas that employees don't need right now but that they might need in the future. The goal is to help employees build and maintain competencies important to companies in general.

How have organizations fared in applying this formula?

In terms of the *partnership relationships,* today's companies are moving in this direction. Conceptually, employees like the idea of greater involvement in decisions. But teams and empowerment programs, the most popular approaches to this new partnership, may not be the right building blocks for creating a new kind of loyalty with survivors of downsizing. To use a medical analogy, teams and greater participation are proven cures for some management ills, but loyalty may not be one of them.

Well-run teams may generate greater numbers of ideas and better-quality ideas. They may also speed implementation of many of these ideas. And they can give employees a greater voice in decisions. But employee loyalty in the past was built on lifetime employment and a sense of family within the company, the most important representative of which was the father figure of the boss. The boss was a protector, someone who helped workers deal with job problems or career problems or even personal problems. Unless employees failed to do the work they were assigned, they had job security, and jobs were so structured that it was clear to a boss when an employee didn't do her job well.

Teams may provide a sense of family, assuming the members are amiable and work well together (which isn't something that automatically comes with teaming), but in organizations designed around teams, there is no boss as such. And in teams, work is not so clear-cut that it is possible to determine without a doubt who is being carried by the team and who is carrying his weight and maybe more.

Furthermore, at a time when survivors of downsizing want to think they can secure their futures with their existing companies by working harder than they ever did before, there is an overwhelming fear among employees that teams and empowerment efforts will make it harder to make decisions and get the work done, Hay has found. They worry that, with responsibilities blurred in these restructured organizations, they can be blamed for lack of team success. And if the team accomplishes its mission, these employees believe they are unlikely to get the credit they deserve.

Looking at the *compensation and benefits area,* variable pay plans work on the assumption that the only thing that really motivates is money, but pay infrequently is at the top of key rewards employees want from work. Interesting work and a job that allows achievement and matches abilities are as or more important, according to Hay Associates.

Furthermore, variable pay rarely makes up more than a minor part of a worker's paycheck—no more than, say, 7 or 8 percent of base salary, which makes me wonder to what extent it can increase motivation or commitment to the company.

Maybe the biggest problem with the use of pay plans to increase commitment and address the problem of lost loyalty may be the difficulty in showing a relationship between worker efforts and an increase in the performance measures used to determine the bonus or incentive pay. Where the linkages aren't clear, monetary incentive systems aren't likely to motivate or establish the commitment to the company that will replace loyalty. And in a survey by Towers Perrin, a little more than half of the group surveyed did not see a strong connection between pay and performance at their companies.

The study by Towers Perrin found that employees had pretty much bought into the new relationship between them and management but doubted how well senior management could deliver on its side of the bargain. The employees said they were willing to take the initiative and actively seek ways to grow the business. But only slightly more than half of those surveyed felt their companies were responsive to changing employee needs, which I believe includes work and family initiatives.

Addressing employees' off-hour needs can foster workers' commitment to their jobs during office hours. But work and family benefits have to go beyond flexible work hours and work-sharing programs to include counseling through life's crises, such as dealing with a parent with Alzheimer's disease or a teenager with a drug problem, as well as help in dealing with life's more predictable situations—finding child care for a toddler, needing time off to take a child to his first day at school, or going for counseling following the death of a parent.

Employee assistance programs can help meet these needs, but most have not yet incorporated procedures that allow managers to recognize early the existence of problems.

On the issue of *employability*, it seems to be more popular to talk about it than to do anything. The objective is to train and educate workers to fulfill new roles within their current organization or in different companies should they lose their current jobs. The 1995 American Management Association's study on downsizing, however, shows that 33 percent of companies decreased training budgets after downsizing. This is sad, since the same study shows a strong correlation between increased training budgets and increased profits and productivity after workforce reductions. However, only 25 percent of those businesses surveyed increased their training budgets after a downsizing.

Training also occurs through lateral moves and the reassigning of responsibilities previously handled by those who were downsized. The new responsibilities, however, infrequently come with a new title or raise. It can get worse. Consider what happened to Corrina, an administrative assistant at a chemical producer in the Southwest.

When her boss was laid off, Corrina was called into the office of the division manager. "Unfortunately, we had to let go several managers," Chet told her. "I know Arnold thought well of your abilities, so I know I can safely put many of the assignments he handled in your hands. You're much more familiar with these reports and the status of these other projects," Chet told her, dumping a stack of folders into her hands. "I have to focus my attention on gaining a bigger market share for our product, or we'll all be on the streets."

"On the streets . . . I hope he's exaggerating," Corrina thought as she left Chet's office. "I don't have enough money in the bank to be laid off." Clearly the only way she could ensure her own employment, she told herself, was to take on as much work as possible—to make herself indispensable. Which is what she did.

Pretty soon the only thing that Corrina wasn't doing that her former boss had done was to get a paycheck as large as his. Chet was very happy with her performance, which is why he called her into his office six months later. He wanted to assure her of how well she had done, but he also wanted to tell her that her job would change significantly in the next month. An improvement in sales had enabled him to replace Arnold, and this new manager would be taking over in four weeks. Chet expected Corrina to help her new boss get settled in and familiarized with the work—work she had been doing for almost a year.

I don't need to tell you that the news severely distressed Corrina, who had hoped for a promotion once the situation at the company had improved. The information also demoralized her pals, who thought she deserved the promotion, and Corrina almost immediately after her meeting with Chet dusted off her résumé and was out job hunting. Her new boss was in his position less than a month when Corrina quit to be assistant manager at another company in the same building.

While employees don't want to job-hop, they will move when they have no evidence to show that loyalty is a two-way street—that is, that their commitment to the organization is matched by a commitment by the organization to show its appreciation to its employees when it can. They'll also job-hop if they are insecure about their current position. Employees may accept the need to lay off people because of sagging corporate finances, and they will work hard to try to help the company turn around, but if they don't see their efforts appreciated or if they feel that their job is in jeopardy, they'll jump ship as soon as they can.

Incidentally, Corrina is representative of many office professionals who have found themselves doing the work of former bosses who were laid off. They are developing new management skills that they might not otherwise have gained. On the other hand, the majority have assumed the additional work normally associated with a promotion without the title, raise, or benefits that should go with it. And should the company decide to fill the position that the office professional is currently performing on a temporary basis, it is more likely that the company will go outside to get a person to fill the vacancy than that it will give the office professional the chance for advancement.

Employment Contracts

A new development is the use of contracts with employees where once they didn't exist to ensure that employees hired stay for some length of time rather than job-hop. A wry commentary on a business community in which reports on downsizing are a daily phenomenon is that many mid-size businesses, concerned that they are just another stop on someone's career path, are contracting with more managers and technical experts and even some workers, demanding a minimum of three to five years, the time it takes for an employer to regain its hiring investment.

It's understandable. Given the background of corporate restructuring, even those people who have been identified as on a fast track are willing to change companies to ensure job secur- ity—usually to a smaller company. If the first company was a multinational, the new one is usually a mid-size business with no global extensions. These smaller businesses may not have the same industry recognition, but the chances of a major restructur- ing are slimmer. Consequently, cutbacks are less likely. And ca- reer advancement is more possible because they aren't already management heavy.

The Balancing Act

How can we address your need for employees who are willing to commit for the long term to an organization and give it their all, even if that organization can no longer promise lifetime em- ployment? Related to this, how can you overcome the feelings of animosity toward the organization felt by the survivors of downsizings?

Employees owe their employers a good day's work for a good day's pay. Employees have to accept that this won't guar- antee job security, but, on the other hand, it may increase their marketability if they use every moment to build their skills, abili- ties, and knowledge.

You, in turn, need to create a work environment in which employees want to contribute and do good work, that helps them to accept teams and other new work arrangements, and that contributes to the rebuilding of a sense of community.

The old promises no longer obtain, but you can give your employees the career guidance that the assessment centers, structured career tracks, and succession programs of old offered. You can provide the help that these programs of the past offered fast-track employees by:

• *Helping your employees set career goals and action plans for achieving these.* Responsibility for one's career now rests with the individual. But you can help your employees determine where they want to go and create a road map to help them get there. That map may not be limited to positions within your own orga- nization, and you have to accept the fact that you may lose an ambitious employee. But you will have the benefit of a highly motivated employee so long as the individual works for you.

• *Finding assignments that will help your employees move in the right direction.* Your employees' growth can be a measure of your managerial effectiveness in finding suitable tasks that will grow their skills.

Like the ladders offered by those old career track and succession programs, assignments that will grow your employees' marketable skills, most importantly in areas related to the career objectives they've identified, can be made available. And, as in the old assessment centers, you can review with your employees their progress in these assignments to help them fine-tune their strengths and get greater insights into skill areas that still need work.

• *Being a guide through the political byways.* The old succession programs and structured career tracks addressed this need. You can replace them by assuming the role of mentor to one or two employees whom you've identified as fast-trackers. Not only will you be their political adviser, but you can help them get their projects successfully completed by sharing your own personal network of contacts within the organization. The project's success will be beneficial not only to the employee but to your organization as well. And you'll be strengthening your own coaching skills.

• *Promoting from within.* Promote on the basis of performance, and always look within the organization for qualified candidates before going outside. Or, sometimes better, where it is possible to do so, rather than promote one individual, redesign the workload of several staff members, giving small raises and new titles to each for assuming the work of the former employee. This way, more than one person gains from the opportunity to earn more money and develop new skills.

Besides adapting the best from these old programs, you can improve the implementation of today's threefold formula for commitment and renewed loyalty through partnerships, work and family initiatives, and employability by:

• *Becoming more aware of the personal needs of your employees.*
Problem-sensing is a technique designed to help you respond to
operational problems in the making by developing your awareness of the work environment around you. It involves asking
several questions:

1. Is something happening that shouldn't?
2. Where is it happening?
3. When is it happening?
4. How long has it been happening?
5. What is its impact on the department? on the corporation?
6. How can you keep the situation from getting out of
   hand?

You can apply this same awareness to your employees' personal needs. Is Marilyn's divorce causing her sleepless nights
and putting so much stress on her that she can't concentrate at
meetings? Does Don seem unnecessarily anxious about the birth
of a new baby? Will Carole have to cancel attendance at her son's
school play if the meeting is late Wednesday afternoon? Just asking the employee if there's a problem may be all the individual
needs to feel you care. Or you may find that the person has a
more serious problem that might need referral to the company's
employee assistance program or to a community group. Ask
yourself:

1. Is someone behaving differently than usual?
2. Where is this behavior evident?
3. When is it evident?
4. How long has it been happening?
5. Is it impacting the individual's usual good nature? Is it
   having a toll on his health?
6. How can I help the person?

• *Setting up department programs that acknowledge the individual, such as sending birthday greetings and congratulations about
weddings and adoptions and allowing time off for bereavement.* One
manager I know arranged to have e-mail messages sent to em-

ployees when a card for a coworker needed to be signed. The cards were kept at a desk just outside his office, and his assistant would make sure that everyone who wanted to do so signed the card and that it was sent on time. Small gatherings were held during the coffee break to celebrate special events in employees' lives—from birthdays to engagements to one employee's new citizenship.

• *Holding department or team meetings in which you can recognize outstanding contributions.* If possible, tangible rewards can be given for exceptional performance, such as cash bonuses, a dinner for two on the company, or a day off. The cost needn't be great so long as the appreciation is sincere.

• *Sharing information with your employees.* Consider holding biweekly operational meetings with employees at which you share information your staff needs to do its work well. If this represents too much of a drain on work time, use other vehicles to communicate with your employees, such as e-mail, corporate newsletters, or messages on a bulletin board.

Most important information about the financial status of the organization should come from you or through you. It's your job to explain the messages to your employees and to help employees understand how the news will affect them.

• *Regularly holding reviews of performance.* Employees are concerned about job security, and regular meetings to discuss their performance give them an opportunity to learn about areas of their performance that need work and about areas where you are delighted with their efforts.

• *Allowing employees to take on more responsibilities as their skills grow.* Recognize that at some point workers deserve to be recognized for doing added work. If money is truly short, then look for other ways to recognize employees until the opportunity to provide financial compensation returns. Be candid with the individual who is given much more responsibility while retaining the same title and salary. And if the higher-paying job opens up again, don't commit the mistake that Corrina's boss did. If someone truly does the job well, then she should get it if and when the job slot can be filled.

• *Setting up controls in the event of partnership programs to*

make responsibilities and accomplishments clear. Since this represents a major concern of survivors of downsizings in today's
team-based organizations, it is an issue you need to address.
Given the move to base compensation in part on team performance, I am slowly coming to the conclusion that team members
may ultimately need some less formal version of job descriptions
to ensure more accurate measurement of their contribution to
the team effort and thereby elicit their more enthusiastic participation in the effort. Until then, you may want to develop forms
that teams can use to identify who is responsible for which assignments and monitor team participation. The form should
show the date the task was given and the date by which the
finished work is due; it should include space for comments
about the quality of the work done. You might want to make
this form visible for all, to motivate team members and to let
employees know that their accomplishments are being recognized.

   • *Keeping an open door.* Even if you can't reassure your employees, you can be available to listen to their concerns, their
insecurities, their sense that their added efforts aren't being appreciated. If they need counseling, help them find it. If they deserve recognition and you've been too busy to give it, apologize
and give it now. If they admit to feelings of stress, either from
the job or from personal problems, you can ease up on their
workload or look for some stress reduction program or the corporate employee assistance program to help them through this
troubling time.

   This kind of personal concern can supplement any corporate work-family initiatives because it, too, tells your employees
that you worry about them as individuals.

   • *Freeing them to try new things, take risks, even make mistakes.*
Greater participation in decisions may challenge workers, generating greater interest and employee commitment. But with
greater participation does, indeed, come greater risks. Your employees will be more willing to accept the new partnership with
you if they know they won't be penalized if the risks don't always work out well. Companies can talk about greater employee
involvement, but if you don't follow up with the freedom to
make mistakes, it won't happen.

• *Following up bad news with explanations.* When financial difficulties force your organization to let employees go, you need to discuss the decision with your employees, acknowledge the hardship caused, and allow employees to ask questions.

When employees think that senior management has it easy, resentment is likely to grow. However, when employees understand the bottom line and see the efforts that management is making to keep costs down, including cuts they themselves are taking, loyalty is bound to be reinforced or to increase.

How you tell them the bad news is as important as what you say. So don't rush through the bad news to get to the next item on the agenda. Don't depersonalize the situation by talking about the individual as "he" or "she" or "them." Refer to the individuals by name to show that they aren't just occupants of desks or positions on the line.

Irene had to announce the decision to close one complete product line. She and a member of the company's employee assistance program met with each of the individuals being let go to explain the situation. But Irene still had to meet with the division's managers and staff and alert them to the information. Afterwards, Irene described to me how upset the decision had made her, her own feelings of loss for these people whom she regarded as friends, and her feelings, too, of failure that she had been unable to find ways to keep the product line alive. Yet at this meeting she was hard as a rock. She made the announcement as if she had never met these individuals in her life, nor had any of the people within the room—among whom, unfortunately, was one team member who would be kept but knew nothing about this until the staff meeting.

As the staff left the room, Helen, the team member, rushed to Irene. She was feeling a number of emotions, including anger that she hadn't been told prior to the meeting, fear that she, too, might be let go, and guilt that she was the only member of the eight-person group to keep her job.

Irene apologized, but Helen never forgot or forgave Irene for that day—and for the feelings she experienced as she sat in that room.

Four years later, when Helen retired, she left with many

good memories but also, she told her coworkers at a party celebrating her departure, some not-so-good memories.

It was unfortunate, because Irene truly felt for those she had
to let go. If only she had shared her own feelings with the group,
they could have felt a sense of community with Irene that could
have improved her relationship with her division. Instead, it led
to some pretty rough months in which morale and productivity
were severely down.

• *Overcoming employee cynicism with honesty.* Employees are
tired of management pap. They want the real lowdown on the
state of the organization so that they can act accordingly, even if
it's as simple as holding off mortgaging the house to build a
third bedroom.

If you know something but can't talk about it, don't tell
your employees what they want to hear. Rather, build their trust
by telling them the truth: You can't comment at this point, but
you will do so as soon as you can. And then be open with them.
If you don't know something, promise to look into the matter
and get back to the person with the question.

Closed doors start rumors and kill morale in a flash.

This is the workable solution to achieving employee loyalty
and commitment in the 1990s. Employees will be loyal to their
work, their careers, and their coworkers, but they have learned
the mistake of depending on their organizations for their careers. Rather, they see the need to be independent, remaining
with their current organization only if they see the present job
as meaningful, which includes providing them with portable
skills, a good relationship with their supervisor or manager, and
an organization that shows it does care about its people despite
the economic realities that sometimes demand tough decisions.

5

Something to Accept: Continuous Improvement Means Continuous Change

Today's organizations have undergone significant change: from the extensive use of teams to greater empowerment of employees, to the introduction of new technologies and their applications, to the creation of more customer-focused products. But we're not done.

To maintain competitive advantage, companies will have to continue to innovate. They'll need to embrace emerging technologies and to respond quickly to a rapidly changing marketplace.

After all, the only thing about business today that is constant is change. And even change has changed to reflect the times.

No longer is change about finding the right or the better way. Rather, change management is about identifying and implementing a better approach and then identifying and implementing a still better one, and so forth and so on. In this respect, the goal of change is continuous improvement—which translates into continuous change.

To see how the level of change in business has grown, you have only to look through an issue of *Business Week* or *Fortune*, with their stories on new TQM initiatives, regulations and laws, downsizings and rightsizings, cultural shifts, efforts at cost containment, programs to integrate a customer service mentality throughout an organization, and acquisitions and divestitures.

Companies are depending on their lower-level managers and employees to produce most of the operational changes that will ensure a successful future. Some companies have initiated empowerment programs to create an environment in which responsibility for major changes, like those related to corporate mission, strategy, vision, and values, still resides with senior management but all others are in the hands of the empowered rank and file. In doing this, these organizations not only are responding to the demand for greater participation in decisions but also are attempting to create an entire organization of successful change agents.

Unfortunately, things haven't worked out as planned.

The Problem

Fewer ideas for change have reached the implementation stage than ever anticipated. And those ideas that have been implemented have generated disappointing results.

Aside from not generating the kind of change activity expected, in some companies experiencing shortfalls in sales or diminishing market share, the situation has deteriorated into a finger-pointing game. Senior management blames primarily a lack of direction from lower-level managers, who, they say, not only aren't initiating change themselves but also are discouraging employees from being innovators, even disparaging the efforts of senior management to transform the company. Senior management accuses lower-level managers of an unwillingness to take the risks that are always a part of change.

On the other hand, lower-level managers blame those in senior management because they haven't provided critical training, resources (like money and people), and a process that will support change initiatives. Yes, they admit, almost half of change initiatives are outright failures. But that's because of bureaucrats in key positions who by nature can't accept change, tight budgets that leave very little money for trying something new, job and time pressures that leave little opportunity for idea development and implementation, and resistance within the organization—even from within the actual teams created to bring about the change—from people who feel threatened by change.

And so the blame game goes, a game in which no one can win—and everyone can lose.

The failure of your organization to change with the times can cost it customers, market share, productivity, or key talent. For your department, it could be the loss of good ideas and staff who either are laid off or leave on their own to set up their own small businesses where they can profit from their ideas.

WIIFM

For you, resisting change can mean a lost opportunity to influence the nature of the change in your organization; the best way to secure your vision of the future is to invent it yourself. You need to empower yourself and your employees to be pioneers—to put some adventure into your workday by identifying new ways of making profits or saving expenses.

The days are gone when you can wait for directions from others. You have to figure out for yourself what your organization needs, then work to see that it gets it. You can't expect a handbook with carefully dilineated instructions on what you're to do. Your new role is to be both a change enabler, supportive of change initiatives of employees and peers, and a change agent, on the lookout for new products, services, or ways of doing the work. You don't want to be perceived as a manager who sits back and lets others address this competitive issue.

Your failure to accept your responsibility to initiate change while other managers in your organization accept it could derail your career.

The Corporate Couch Potato

When a major midwestern insurance company had to choose which of two managers it would promote to division head of a growing new business, that one candidate had a successful track record in heading up change efforts clearly had an impact on the final decision.

Although Mark and Terry worked in different parts of the organization, coincidentally they had both been given similar mandates: improve the productivity of their downsized organizations. Neither Mark's underwriting department nor Terry's claims department could be further downsized; management felt only that both could be more customer-focused and operate more efficiently. Despite the downsizings only a short time before, the atmospheres in both departments were too relaxed and laid back.

Mark ignored the mandate, whereas Terry didn't. While Terry was holding meetings with her team to identify ways the group could complete the work more quickly and better satisfy customer needs, Mark was focused on the day-to-day. He felt he had enough to do without adding new projects because management *thought* there were greater efficiencies possible. After all, no one's job was on the line.

It never occurred to Mark to ask his staff for suggestions about how the risk reports could be processed more quickly. If he had, he would have learned that the staff had wanted for some time to review operating procedures because it felt there were several redundant steps in the process and other steps that should be incorporated to improve the accuracy of the work.

Terry's meeting with her staff led to identification of four steps that the staff could take to speed up its work. I can't say that there wasn't any internal resistance to the changes—there was—but Terry had the support of the majority of the group, and those employees were able to convince the opposition to try out the new system. It worked, and customers were delighted at the speed with which claims were now processed.

That Terry and her staff were successful clearly influenced management. But that Mark hadn't even tried influenced senior management even more, since the position that both were candidates for demanded someone who could be comfortable when it wasn't "business as usual."

The surest path to advancement today comes from a willingness to initiate change and to accept the risks associated with it.

Back to the Basics

Until the last decade or so, change was generally top-down–led. There were managers—mostly mavericks—who came up with inventive ideas for products or solutions to problems and brought them to top management's attention. And there were suggestion systems that offered managers and employees an opportunity to share their ideas and gain financial rewards for them—a percentage of the savings or profits. But most ideas came from atop the pyramid.

The world wasn't as fast-paced as it is today, so this pace of change was possible. And because the directives came from the very highest levels of the organization, there was a sense of urgency associated with them that ensured their implementation. All a manager had to say was, "Mr. Big wants . . . ," and she was assured of support from all within the organization.

Senior management would frequently contract with an outside consulting firm to study an operating area, and it would keep the consulting firm's conclusions under wraps until it was ready to unveil them, usually with very specific directions for implementation.

Communicate, Communicate, Communicate

Implementation was the responsibility of lower-level managers. Many supervisors involved their employees in the implementation planning because they saw the common sense in participative management. Employees were closer to the work. And their involvement encouraged buy-in into the plans and increased the likelihood that the plans would be achieved. So these more progressive managers encouraged employees to voice their ideas.

Lower-level managers generally followed a single rule of thumb to encourage employees to support change efforts: communicate, communicate, communicate. They did this in several ways:

- *They provided advance information.* Advance notice helped employees to accept the change when it came, particularly if the notice included information on how the change would benefit them (WIIFT or *What's In It for Them*).

Even with negative change, advance notice and continuous communication were proven to discourage foot-dragging. (Parenthetically, two-way communication also was practiced with managerial peers to gain their cooperation. It was almost as if lower-level managers came together to avert problems; after all, if one supervisor failed to carry his share of the change, the entire program might not succeed.)

- *They gave employees a chance to vent.* When a change had a negative impact on the employees, managers found that it paid to give them an opportunity to air their feelings. Ignoring them only encouraged them to go underground.

- *They asked for employee suggestions to ensure successful implementation.* This was the most critical step, since it encouraged employee buy-in into the plan and minimized resistance. Besides, employees were able to contribute insights from their own work experiences that could improve the change action plan. And employees who felt ownership with the plan had been found to work harder to make it a success.

Throughout, these lower-level managers learned to be open to employees' ideas, not only to get help with the plan but because, by being open-minded, they were role-modeling behaviors they also expected of their employees.

Those managers who practiced these steps were able to excite their employees about change, reduce resistance, and create a culture within their department that allowed innovations to succeed.

While these steps minimized resistance to change, they did not answer the need for a way to utilize the full competence—the skills, abilities, and knowledge—of managers and staffs. It took the transformation to team structures—in the 1970s, quality circles (QCs); in the 1980s, teams formed to promote total quality; in the 1990s, team management—to open the door for that level of creativity.

Fad Solutions

Change today comes primarily through teams. This isn't to say that an individual can't come up with and implement an idea for a new product or service or for a more efficient or effective way to work. It's just that teams are seen as more likely to identify and implement ideas because in today's pared-down organizations, a team can often do more than one individual can; several individuals working together are likely to generate more and better quality ideas than someone concentrating on the same problem on his own; and in today's organizations problems and opportunities require insights from various disciplines and so are best handled by groups of individuals who represent these different functions.

So teams can be enormously successful change agents. However, not all teams succeed at change. That became evident as early as the 1970s in which companies found some QCs very helpful in identifying and solving problems and others less so.

Even with a clear focus and direction and good leadership, teams fail sometimes because they base their conclusions on assumptions, not facts, and focus on symptoms, not root causes. Consequently, the problems they're addressing recur.

Another problem with today's change efforts is that teams or individuals seem too often to grab hold of an idea that reflects more the latest cover story on a weekly business magazine than corporate needs. Jed, a warehousing manager, is guilty of this all the time.

Improving Warehousing Productivity

Jed had heard about plans to introduce a new line of product. For the warehouse to contend with the added shipments, Jed would have to increase worker productivity. He couldn't hire more employees; there was a hiring freeze throughout the plant. What could he do?

On his commute home, while reading an issue of *Business Week*, he saw a story about a company that had instituted a productivity improvement program that had been very successful. "That's my answer," he thought. Two days later, as workers entered the warehouse, they found signs taped to the walls and notices on every surface announcing a new program. Employees could earn time off based on the number of shipments above standard they moved during the day. There was some confusion at first among the workers about how points would be distributed among the eight employees, but Jed assured the team he would work out any bugs in the program as they went along. And on the surface, the program seemed to work. Soon cartons were flying out of the warehouse onto the loading docks. Two weeks into the program, however, Jed discovered some major flaws.

The most immediate problem was that one of Jed's workers—of course, one of his least productive—had tabulated the amount of free time available and wanted his fair share at the same time as another of Jed's warehouse employees—the most productive—wanted his. Jed could let both off, but having two employees away at the same time would create shipping problems. But maybe more serious was the concern of the human resources department that Jed's program had set a precedent; soon every employee in the organization would want time off if he or she exceeded work standards. But the worst problem was that several cartons had been mistakenly shipped to the wrong customer. They could be returned, but in the meantime the three cartons that the customer desperately needed couldn't be located.

Jed knew he would have to discontinue the incentive program, but he wondered what he could do instead to maintain the higher level of productivity he had achieved. As he was thinking, he was thumbing through a trade magazine. There, on page 36 in the third paragraph of the August issue was his answer. A warehouse manager had increased productivity through a values program that promoted an assortment of critical values, from risk taking to conscientiousness. Duplicating the values listed on page 37 took only a few minutes. Jed had these printed on tiny cards that he distributed to each of his team members. Within a few days, every staff member had on his desk one of the laminated cards and a notice about the new values program.

Jed would stop different workers and ask what the department's values were, just as he had read that the other manager had done. And the worker would repeat them and earn $25 for naming all ten. The program was cutting into Jed's budget, but he felt the long-term benefits would justify the variance in expenses.

After a while, Jed began to notice that while the team could repeat all the values, they weren't necessarily practicing them. And those with the best memories also seemed to be the worst offenders. "What should I do now?" he wondered.

The cover of *Fortune* offered an answer. There Jed found a story about how to use the fun of competition to increase productivity. Out went the cards; in came a large chart on which each employee's name appeared. The employee who moved the most cartons during the month would get a free dinner for two at one of the more luxurious restaurants in town.

A few back injuries later, this idea, too, was shelved.

Maybe worse, over time, performance began to seriously decline as employees grew tired of going from one new program to another. Jed lost his staff's respect and their interest. After all, this week it might be an internal customer-focused survey—which the workers actually thought was a good idea—but by the next week Jed might have dropped the survey idea and sent a memo asking staff members to complete a major study of what new technology they would need to more quickly move materials through the warehouse.

A Publications Approach to Change

Jed's behavior reflects that of his company, one of many today that seem to move from one fad to another. Many create teams of managers to investigate the worth of these programs for their organizations, but many more bypass any initial research. Instead, they quickly implement a program on the assumption that the business press has an uncanny ability to identify those factors that are most critical to competitive success. They don't question the fit of the program with their culture, their organization, their strategy, or their marketplace. It seems more important to implement the change quickly than to conduct a realistic assessment of its chances of success. Held in disdain are managers who want to pilot test.

Admittedly, people are pressed, with too much to do and too little time to do it. But too many managers seem to feel that they don't have enough time to do something right but that they will have the time to do it over. They don't realize that an initial failure could cost them any second chance with this change or with any future change they try to initiate.

But at least there is substance to the effort. Some change initiatives tied to popular buzzwords aren't even backed with real action plans. Lip service is given to words like total quality, value-added service, or customer enfranchisement—and nothing more. It's as if the people behind the change effort believe that talking about the change will make it so.

The Balancing Act

What can we take from the past and from the present to make change management more successful in today's companies?

The Issue of Teams

Because change management today is often done through change teams (primarily cross-functional teams), you need team leaders who are skilled at planning, communication, follow-through, and follow-up—in other words, good team managers. If you wish to attempt change through teams, these points are important to remember:

• *Team change efforts need sponsorship.* If the team gets buy-in from someone in senior management who sees the change as contributing directly to his operation, the team is more likely to get the resources it needs to implement its idea.

A sponsor is someone who is willing to support the project throughout, from the first session in which mission is agreed on, through problem solving and planning, resource allocations (either providing necessary resources himself or herself or using his or her internal network to do so), and final recommendations, speaking out for the change in the higher circles of the organization.

• *Change teams need a network of supporters.* Besides the support of the sponsor (the team's "Mr. Big"), the group should have the cooperation of those in key positions. As change advocates, they can make it easier for you to sell your change team's plan to the larger group—and in a shorter period of time.

• *Change teams need the right mix of people.* You need both creative out-of-the-box thinkers *and* more traditional problem solvers who can make the hotshot ideators' ideas work.

The ideation process itself should be built not on assumptions but on facts, gathered after defining the team's mission. The consultants of the 1960s, 1970s, and 1980s relied on objective information gathered rather than on long-held but often false assumptions about a situation. So should your team.

Often an analysis of the facts can enable a team to break out of the thinking ruts that too often lead to treatment of the symptoms, not the root causes of the problem, and consequently set the stage for a recurrence of a problem.

• *Change team leaders need to plan for resistance from within.* Because consensus-driven teams are composed of empowered team members, you as a team leader need to prepare for resistance to your ideas from within the team during idea development. You should also have a plan to handle opposition from outside once the idea is being implemented.

Your team members are no different from people not on the team. They will consider every proposal on the table from the perspective of what they might lose rather than what they might have to gain. Critical to your leadership role, therefore, will be drawing a positive picture of the outcomes to overcome this natural defensive behavior.

Members of a team may want different levels of change, too. Some members may accept their mission with excitement and enthusiasm, while others will act as if anchors are tied to their legs. As leader of a change team, your objective is to increase the acceptance to change of the least ready members, because their pace actually will influence the total pace.

To move the team along, you'll have to utilize your coaching and counseling skills. But you'll have to be tactful in pressing for action, because too much pressure could be seen by members as leader domination, generating resistance.

Sometimes resistance has less to do with the idea being promoted than with the team leader's management style. Leaders who interrupt others with opinions different from theirs or otherwise dominate and allow others to dominate sessions are likely to meet member resistance from the first day. The rebellion may be passive, in the form of missed meetings, tardiness, and undone team assignments, or more aggressive, with members who have felt slighted grinding their heels in and refusing to go along with the rest of the group.

Planning for Change

Through the change planning process, there will be questions you will need to answer. You have to plan your answers as you would any task. Typical questions include these:

- What is our mission or goal?
- What resources (equipment, people, money) will we need, and how will we get these?
- By when do we expect to complete implementation of our change?
- If change will come in stages, what will be the timetable?
- What are the outcomes of each stage of the change plan?
- Who should be involved in each step?
- How will we measure success? (You'll want specific, measurable, realistic, time-related goals.)
- What alternative steps can we take (Plan B) if Plan A fails?
- Whose support is needed? How do we handle the bureaucratic red-tapers and other resistance?

Managing the Change Effort

Whether you are initiating change via a team or on your own or are a team sponsor, you will need to:

- *Make a compelling case for change.* Besides the who, what, and where associated with the change, you need to explain the why—maybe again and again and again.

Use every vehicle to share your mission: big or small meetings, memos, e-mail, the corporate newsletter, lunch dates with colleagues. Communicate the vision in terms that will be understood by the listener.

Many change experts attribute the failure of so many change initiatives today to a lack of sense of urgency about the need to change. They suggest that there is a complacency in some organizations, due in part to postdownsizing communications designed to reassure managers and employees and in part to the natural human tendency for people to see and hear what they want—which is that "things aren't too bad."

I think this is part of the problem. But I also believe that there is too much emphasis on the who, what, and where and too little on the why about change. Managers of the 1960s, 1970s, and 1980s were right: Communicate, communicate, communicate. You can never assume that the reasons for a change are obvious to those whose support you need. Maybe the reasons are obvious to you, and maybe they are obvious to members of your change team, but they may not be obvious to others.

If a company is in trouble and you want to get more employee involvement in change efforts, it's critical that you make a strong case for employee participation and support of change efforts. But in doing this, you need to balance a sense of urgency with feelings of personal confidence that the employees are capable of turning the situation around. Creativity and risk taking are less likely in an environment of fear. And talented staff— those individuals most likely to lead change initiatives—will seek employment elsewhere rather than stay on a potentially sinking ship.

- *Be tolerant of mistakes.* Change means risk. This means that mistakes will be made. But your message, in the face of mistakes, must be that the only failure you're concerned about is the failure to try anything at all.

Besides, problems routinely occur with any change initiative. Solving those problems may generate other problems, which will cause further problems. This is just the nature of change. All you can do is address each problem calmly as it occurs.

• *Work to create short-term wins.* Develop your change initiative to achieve visible performance improvements as early evidence that the change will work. And find ways to recognize and reward the employees behind these quick wins.

The importance of these short-term successes can't be overestimated. Eyes are always on change efforts. And opponents of change will be looking for proof that an idea won't work. But it's hard to argue with success.

It's tougher to justify change on the basis of soft data—things like improved morale, trust, loyalty, stress levels, or job satisfaction—than of hard data—like productivity increases, bigger market share, faster delivery, higher customer satisfaction indices, shorter product development cycles, and high initial sales. Once these hard-data gains are achieved, build on them. This keeps the momentum of the change effort going, which will give you an opportunity to change other elements (like structure or systems) that don't fit well with the initial change.

Overcoming Resistance

The biggest problem with any change effort is overcoming resistance to implementation. Too many managers still think that a memo about a new program or procedure or a brief announcement about a shift in directions is sufficient to get employee buy-in into the change. Not so.

Memos and fine speeches aren't sufficient to overcome resistance. And overcoming resistance is the biggest barrier to change. That's why the change plan should include action steps to overcome resistance. After all, almost one half of all change initiatives fail because of staff resistance during implementation.

It has been estimated that on average about 20 percent of people presented with a change will accept it, another 50 percent will sit on the fence until they have reason to support or obstruct a change, and 30 percent will drag their feet, even sabotage the effort. Your resistance plan should focus on convincing the 50 percent; attention given to the 30 percent who have already decided against the change is wasted.

To overcome resistance, you should:

• *Be empathic.* Change always generates an emotional reaction. People will support your change effort only if you demonstrate you care. That involves listening to their concerns and responding to them. Remember how managers in the 1970s and 1980s listened to their employees' concerns about implementation?

You need to encourage a free flow of information to determine what is worrying an employee who is resistant to some change you are attempting to implement. To do that, you need to ask open-ended questions that can't be answered with a "yes" or "no" but rather allow the individual to tell you what he thinks; you need to demonstrate your interest in the person's viewpoint by remaining silent when he speaks and nodding your head, not to say that you agree but rather that you heard what he said and are interested in more, and by restating or reflecting what you heard, both the facts and the emotions expressed.

You won't get this kind of exchange if you conduct a one-sided diatribe in which you tell a resister why he *must* accept the change or regularly interrupt the speaker with statements like, "Yeah, but you don't seem to understand that. . . ."

• *Get others involved.* To get their full cooperation, make individuals and teams a part of the change process. "But everything has been decided," you say. Not so. Chances are if you take a close look at a situation, you will find there are ways to include these individuals in some of the final decisions. And as managers learned decades ago, when employees are involved in deciding how to implement changes, those changes become their own changes, and cooperation automatically follows.

• *Give people a chance to say goodbye.* People need time to mourn for the old ways and take ownership of the new. Sometimes, you can help them do this by appealing to their self-interests. Maybe what's in it for them is an opportunity for career advancement, or maybe a more efficient way of getting the work done. Whatever it is, it needs to be clarified. And if training is called for to enable employees to work under changed circumstances, there should be sufficient time for learning the new skills.

• *Get resistance out in the open.* Resistance can be triggered by a number of factors, including fear of loss of job security or control, laziness about learning something new, previous bad experiences with change, failure to see the benefit in change, and comfort with established procedures and policies. In your change efforts, your obligation should be to get this resistance out in the open, where you can address the concerns of the opposition.

Sometimes opposition is justifiable. If so, you'll want to know why so you can adjust the plan accordingly.

• *Choose your first step carefully.* How you begin your change effort may influence the degree of opposition you encounter.

Gradual introduction of change is likely to generate the least opposition, but, once noticed, the change is easily countered; the opposition has time to assemble its arguments against your plan. Often the best strategy is a bold step that gets people's attention and, in the process, frightens off the opposition. You have more chance of seeing your idea implemented.

• *Don't compromise.* Too much flexibility at this stage could send a message to everyone, including that critical 50 percent, that you're not totally committed to the plan.

• *Don't fight; talk it out.* Literature about change often suggests that you need to fight to overcome resistance to change. But you can't get people to accept change by pushing them or pulling them toward it. You've got to get them to want to change.

That's why communication during not only the planning process but also the implementation stage is so critical. The "why" could be a problem that needs to be remedied or an opportunity that offers revenue growth or cost savings or, better still, both.

Of course, even the most worthwhile of changes will generate fear if it will replace what's known, familiar, comfortable, or habitual with what's unknown, unfamiliar, and initially uncomfortable. But understanding exactly what will replace the known can make the transition period bearable and the change itself more acceptable. The managers of the 1960s, 1970s, and 1980s were correct in their insistence in providing those people who were most affected by a change with advance information and ongoing updates about what would be changed, when the change would occur, and whom it would affect.

If you're to get people to accept a change, whatever its nature, your job is to pull them along during the transition phase. That means that you have to clearly define the destination you both will reach when the process is completed.

If you can't reveal all that you know, be honest and explain the situation. Assure your audience that as soon as you know everything and are given the liberty to discuss it, you will do so. In the meantime, refute any rumors you can.

• *Adapt your communications to your resisters.* Consider the kinds of people you work with. There are those who place value on facts, figures, and other data, others who place value on results, still others who will act on faith, and those who are more interested in abstract ideas than the nitty-gritty. To win over these different individuals, you need to know which person is an analyzer, which is more results-focused, and which is more a socializer and then play to each individual's communication style.

Let's say, for instance, you are talking to an analytic type. You might say:

1. "Let me walk you through this change step by step."
2. "Let's look at this change in a logical, systematic way."
3. "Why don't you study it, and I'll get back to you."

If you're talking to a socializer, you might say:

1. "Linda, in marketing, has looked over the proposal and she thinks this is a good approach."

2. "Why don't we discuss your concerns over lunch with some of the employees who have addressed these concerns and overcome them?"
3. "It's important that I get you and your staff involved in this process from the beginning."

If you're talking to the results-oriented, you might disclose:

1. "This will have almost an immediate payoff if we. . . ."
2. "I need only five minutes of your time to explain. . . ."
3. "We have the most practical approach here."

Or if you're talking to a conceptualizer, someone who places more emphasis on ideas and concepts than on facts, results, or emotions, you might say:

1. "Let me explain the basic principles behind the change."
2. "I think we have a very unique approach—something that has never before been applied."
3. "I think you'll find this concept fits well with your own idea about. . . ."

• *Don't underestimate the power of the bureaucrats.* They likely make up a good portion of the 30 percent of the 20-50-30 equation. You won't be able to sell them on the change, but you can monitor their actions and countermove, using the change advocates in your internal network.

• *Establish a reward system.* Recognition for contributions to implementation of the change can speed its acceptance. If possible, tie bonuses or promotions, even high-visibility assignments, to desired outcomes. Even a "thank you" can go a long way.

Incidentally, don't forget to offer similar rewards to members of your change team who went out of their way to move the plan along.

• *Track progress, and measure results.* Initial ideas about what will work and what won't may not always be right.

Throughout the change effort, you should be learning from your mistakes. Discuss with your team or others involved in the change effort what took place, the decisions that were made and the reaons behind those decisions, and what actions should be taken in the future.

- *Know when to call the effort off.* Not every change you lead or support will succeed. There always comes a time when you have to fish or cut bait.

More important than the fact you have to kill a project is how you do it. You don't want to discourage other change efforts by your actions. Don't pretend the failure didn't happen. Rather, address the reason the project is being declared at an end. Share with those involved with you in the project what was learned from the effort. And, most important, discuss with your supporters what will be done differently in the future with change initiatives to increase the odds of their success. Go out on a positive note.

6

Too Much Talk, Too Much E-Mail: Not Much Communication

Communication has always been a critical part of managers' jobs, but never before have we spent so much time at it—talking with members of our work teams and cross-functional teams, with those above and below us on the corporate ladder, and with those outside our organizations and within them and composing and receiving written and electronic communications. This has created for each of us managers one or both of the following situations:

- Stress from trying to keep on top of all the information, making us victims of information overload
- Frustration because, despite so much talk and written communication (on-line now as well as on paper), there doesn't appear to be *real* communication taking place.

In both instances, there isn't a significant improvement in communication, not if you think of communication as a process that begins when you have an idea, information, or a feeling to share and that ends when the person or group to whom the idea, information, or feeling was sent gets the message and responds or reacts in a manner that shows that the message sent was understood or interpreted correctly.

The Problem

Communication has always been a management problem, as suggested by these examples:

• *Lack of listening to employees.* Joel had a good idea for improving one of his company's products, one that would revive a dying sales item, but Cindy, his boss, focused on her lengthy to-do list, misunderstood what he was saying, and discounted the idea. She wasn't listening, and it cost her company major market share.

• *Failure to provide feedback.* Margo talks frequently with all her employees—her good performers and her problem workers—but most of her conversations are about mutual off-hour interests, not work problems. Margo's not as comfortable talking about job performance, which is why it took her several weeks to discuss Jim's work performance with him. She had talked to everyone but Jim about his failure to take initiative until Margo's own boss, seeing Jim sitting quietly in his cubicle reading a book, forced her to meet with him. "If Jim has such free moments," Bob said, "maybe we don't need a full-time employee." Margo needed a full-time employee, and she hoped it would be Jim, so, uncomfortable as it made her feel, after much stalling, she sat down with him to talk about those things he should have been doing but wasn't. In the course of the conversation, Margo discovered that Jim had no idea that she wanted him to take charge of several areas of work or that until now he had felt he was dependent on her for assignments. There was no real problem, only miscommunication about what needed to be done.

• *Focus on our needs, not those of the person with whom we are talking.* Bill often talks to Sam, one of his customers, and Sam frequently mentions problems he is having with his own customers, but Bill is so wrapped up in trying to make a sale to Sam during these meetings that he isn't listening to Sam, whose comments not only could help him close a big deal with Sam but might suggest new products for Bill's company.

- *Disorganized or incomprehensible messages.* Isaac issues lots of memos and holds lots of staff meetings. It's hard to decide how valuable either technique is, because neither the memos nor the meetings are well organized or comprehensible. Individuals leave Isaac's meetings shaking their heads. They know something important was said, but they are apprehensive because they're not sure what it was. His memos just leave individuals confused and, strangely enough, hoping for a staff meeting in which, if they are lucky, they might make head or tail of Isaac's latest directive.

- *Compulsive memo-writing.* Hannah has great ideas and enthusiastically memos—on paper or e-mail—her boss each time she thinks of something. Either the messages are very short or they are very long, several pages of paper or the equivalent. In either case, because Hannah hasn't really thought through her ideas—she puts down the first thoughts that come to her—the ideas are unfinished, and her boss has made no effort to pursue any one of them.

- *Compulsive talking.* Priscilla doesn't rely on the printed word; she talks to her staff, and talks to her staff, and talks some more to her staff. But the messages seem to get lost in all the verbiage. Her instructions to her employees are always so ambiguous that the workers are almost guaranteed to make mistakes in trying to follow them.

- *Writing to impress, not to express.* Ingrid's memos and reports are written to impress the reader, not to communicate. Her memos aren't anywhere near reader-friendly, with their extralong sentences and their unfamiliar words. Consequently, they get lost in their recipients' in-boxes, where they're sandwiched between other papers and languish, despite their critical content.

- *Information overload.* Mary comes into the office each morning, and besides checking her phone, whose mailbox may be full with messages, she has to review all her e-mail messages and a pile of correspondence. Then there are the newsletters and magazines she receives that demand her attention if she is to stay on top of developments in the pharmaceutical industry. Almost every day, she discovers she is several memos behind and has not responded to a request from a colleague or her boss. Her employees misunderstand her lack of response, seeing it as indifference when it simply means that she hasn't yet read their message. Even though she takes home newsletters and magazines each evening to read, along with corporate reports and proposals, and stays late at night to go through her electronic mail, she still has an in-box likely to tumble over with all the paper in it.

- *Lack of facilitation skills.* The cross-functional team that Hal formed to determine the reasons for the high reject rate for one of the plant's products has yet to come up with an action plan, despite the talent represented within the team. During the first few meetings, Hal showed himself quick to criticize ideas he disagreed with, and since then the team's members have become idea-shy.

Management Efforts

In the past, the communication focus was on the lack of clarity of written and oral messages and on the lack of feedback from and the poor listening skills of managers. Today, we have too much information hitting our desks daily (on paper and via electronic mail) and too many meetings in which there is much talk but not as much listening—and in team settings the listening aspect of communication is generally more important than the talking.

Not only do we have new communication problems, but the stakes are higher. Failure to stay abreast of developments in our department, company, or field can mean that we don't take the necessary steps to prevent situations from becoming problems, work collaboratively with our colleagues, or keep our department's efforts competitive with those of other companies in our industry.

In team settings, a leader's domination of a meeting or failure to listen with an open mind to others' ideas can destroy the collaboration so critical to achieving the team's purpose or mission. The inability of leaders to prevent some members from putting down the contributions of shyer colleagues can mean that a new product doesn't fly or that high operating costs price a product out of the market. Members of cross-functional teams who don't communicate openly—that is, who keep to themselves information about the undiscussables (like the sacred cows that dwell within their operating areas) or past department efforts that failed—contribute to lack of trust within the team and consequently create a self-defeating team environment.

WIIFM

If you want a reason to become a more effective communicator, consider this: A major demotivator in organizations is poor communication. When you don't listen to employees' ideas, problems, or concerns in one-on-one and group meetings, you're affecting their view of the work environment. This, in turn, impacts their level of motivation, as Douglas McGregor, in *The Human Side of Enterprise* noted. Or remember Abraham Maslow and his emphasis on self-esteem? He found that employees believe that we don't care about them when we don't listen to their ideas—which demotivates them.

Demotivation, in turn, causes low morale, high absenteeism and turnover, and shoddy productivity, not to mention rework and rejects.

As many as 75 percent of the mistakes that occur in the workplace are due to ineffective communication. Poor communication can cost time and money, which can affect your department's bottom line. And in today's budget-conscious workplaces, I don't think I need to remind you about how closely your career—even your job—is tied to your department's bottom line.

In cross-functional teams, when you dominate meetings or by your actions as team leader fail to encourage participation by all, you demotivate the team's members, which can undermine the team's mission. When you contribute to your colleagues' information overload by sending unnecessary or incomprehensible e-mail or rambling phone mail, you're becoming an irritation to them that could cost you their support when you most need it. And if you don't learn how to manage incoming e-mail, phone mail, correspondence, and other information, you can find yourself unaware of important developments that can help you do your job better, which may mean that you will be left behind in the career competition.

"I don't need to become an effective communicator," you say. "I already am." Maybe. But most managers aren't as good as they think. Consider the results of a telephone survey by *Getting Results . . . For the Hands-On Manager,* which identified a number of workplace communications problems, especially in the clarity of managers' communications, supervisors' receptiveness and responsiveness to employees' ideas, and the adequacy of managerial feedback.

The truth is, we all tend to take our communication ability for granted, like breathing. The fact is that most of us have never learned to communicate as well as we could because we have never really given any attention to the development of good communication skills. Which is what I'm suggesting you do.

Back to the Basics

Much of the literature of the past on communication focuses on the obstacles to good comunication, like lack of a clear message, poor timing, inadequate listening skills, poor selection of the means by which the message was communicated (in writing or orally), cultural and language barriers, differences in perception (due to differences in learning styles, age, gender, or education), and use of emotionally loaded words or slogans.

Barriers to Good Communication

Communication is a process, and traditionally the focus has been on that process and the barriers that can exist between the sender and the receiver of a message. Let's look at the sequence of events: The sender creates the message; the sender decides on the best channel for sending it (that is, whether to tell the other party or to write out the message); the sender imparts the message; and the receiver of the message interprets the message. The emphasis in the past was on this last step and on the impact that the filters of timing, perception, cultural or educational background, and similar factors could have on the communication. This included the issue of listening. Managers were taught to get feedback from the recipient to ensure that the message had been received and understood.

Let's look at some instances in which filters might impede communication:

• *Poor timing.* A manager stops an employee on Friday evening as the employee is leaving and gives him detailed instructions about a job he is to begin the first thing Monday morning.

• *Language problems.* Clara, a manager, sends a multiple-page memo to workers for whom English is a second language. It never occurred to her that her Hispanic employees, who make up about two-thirds of the plant's employees, would have a hard time reading the message and that consequently the plant's new safety procedures would not be followed. She had carefully drafted and distributed the in-depth memo about new operating procedures, but it went unread. Once she became aware of the problem, she changed communication channels. Instead of writing to her workers, she held staff meetings at which she discussed new operating procedures and other issues they needed to be aware of.

• *Inappropriate channels.* A sales manager held meetings with customer and sales staffs to discuss technical changes to his firm's line of microwaves. Feedback suggested that staff had problems both understanding the virtues of these changes and recalling them at the point of customer contact. So the sales manager decided to distribute product updates following any product changes. These handouts described the changes and their values to the customer. Distribution of these market sheets was followed by staff meetings to allow reps to ask further questions as well as to share with the sales manager any recent customer reactions to the company's product line that might suggest new product offerings or help in marketing the product.

• *Emotions.* A simple question like "When do you think you'll finish that job?" can trigger in an employee/receiver an assortment of feelings, depending on his past relationship with the supervisor or manager. If the employee has had performance problems in the past but they have been resolved, the question might suggest to the reformed worker that the manager has yet to forgive or forget the previous work history. Thus the work relationship declines.

• *Different perceptions.* Perceptions stem from a variety of factors—age and gender, education, past work history. Many older managers find it harder in team meetings to involve their employees in the decision-making process. As their organization has moved to horizontal management, they have had to develop a more democratic style of communication, and some are unable to put aside their years spent working in an autocratic work environment to truly hear—that is, to objectively listen to—the ideas of their workers.

Measuring the Quality of Your Communication

An interesting way of measuring the quality of communication was described by Edward L. Levine, writing in *Supervisory Management* magazine. The measurement tool is based on work by the social psychologist R. F. Bales, and it looks at one-on-one communication on task acomplishments and social-emotional issues. Task accomplishments are defined as those aspects of the communication aimed at producing outputs from the meeting (e.g., solutions to problems, new work procedures). Social-emotional issues are related to the interpersonal relationship between employee and supervisor. Negative social-emotional communications include interrupting an employee or referring to his idea as "dumb."

The tool itself is a chart divided into two parts. On it the manager indicates the number of times she gave suggestions, opinions, and information and asked for suggestions, opinions, and information. There is also a section on which the number of times the employee did the same is recorded. There is also room to tally the number of instances of silence between the two.

It's not a simple chart to maintain during a conversation, but it does give some indication of the number of occasions in which the manager dominates a discussion or the number of long silences. Using it or something equivalent can help you determine the quality of the interaction between you and an employee. Obviously, the most productive conversations you have with employees are those made up of an equal number of comments initiated by you and the employee, with few moments of silence and, most important, lots of suggestions from the employee.

Listening got lots of attention in the past; indeed, it continues to be seen as more important than the communication side. The focus has always been on teaching managers how to listen better by learning how not to let distractions—the phone, unexpected visitors, or the paperwork on their desks—prevent them from hearing what is being said; how to avoid allowing their own prejudices about the speaker or his or her style of address to influence their opinion about what he or she has said; how to keep from interrupting no matter how much they either disagree with the remarks or are enthusiastic about what they are hearing; and how to avoid thinking about how to rebut what is being said while the other party is speaking so that they don't hear all that is being said. Maybe most important, managers have always been taught the value of empathic listening, that is, the willingness to change their opinion based on what they hear—clearly an important communication skill in today's more collaborative workplace.

Finally, in helping managers with their listening skills, traditional management spoke about the 80/20 rule, something you'll see often mentioned in this book. It simply means that you shouldn't dominate conversations in group settings or one on one. Twenty percent of your time should be spent talking, and the remaining 80 should be spent listening; that's the most valuable time in any conversation.

To help managers discover if they dominate conversations and to teach them to improve the flow of conversation with employees, one educator has recommended that they flowchart their conversations with employees. The goal is to identify how often the manager interrupts the employee. The idea behind the flowchart is that an effective one-on-one communication session is marked by lots of talking on the part of both people.

Written Communication

Written communication has received almost as much attention as oral communication.

Since clarity of communication begins with organizing one's thoughts, managers have long been taught to think through what they plan to say before putting words to paper. If they can't do that, before beginning to write, they should start by jotting down a few words, phrases, or other notes to help organize their thinking. Outlining is also helpful, particularly for long reports or memos.

Such an outline breaks down the document into a lead sentence; separate paragraphs, each for a different thought; introductory sentences for each paragraph to position it within the main document and allow for scanning; and a closing or summary statement at the end.

Clarity is critical to written communication, which means that your intention is to communicate a message, not to impress your reader with your use of language or vocabulary. Fancy vocabularies and long sentences might have impressed your high school English teacher, but they lead only to confusion in the business world. Better to use shorter, more familiar words. And get to the point. Managers don't have the time to write long memos unless the contents demand it, and their readers don't have the time to read long memos and reports unless the content requires it.

Most important, managers have been told to question each piece of paper they send to another: Is the memo needed? Does the report have to be distributed to every member of the department or to each employee?

Fad Solutions

In today's flatter organizations, we can send messages directly to those we want to receive them. We don't have to go up and down the organizational pyramid to get the information we want, information that might become confused en route.

With the help of e-mail, we can also communicate faster—which means improved communication between our own supervisors, colleagues, or employees and us, not to mention our customers, suppliers, and others with whom we need to stay in touch.

But many people have yet to master the use of electronic mail. Some are still wrestling with the proper use of voice mail. I'm talking not just about which keys on the phone to press or icons to click in a software program but about when and how to use that new technology most effectively. Excessive use of phone mail and e-mail has contributed to the information overload many of us are experiencing.

Voice Mail

Let's start with the simpler technology—voice mail. With voice mail, if the person isn't there, you can leave a voice mail message. If your question is a simple one, you can leave your query on the party's voice mail, and she can leave a reply on your machine if you aren't around to pick up the phone when she calls back. This makes it easier to send quick messages; the game of telephone tag may not have disappeared entirely, but the number of instances in which it occurs have been reduced.

Still, there are problems with voice mail. Have you ever come into the office and pressed "Listen" on your phone, then heard a long and rambling message from a colleague, client, or boss? Do you leave equally long, detailed messages for your staff? Many managers, in a rush to get work done, send job instructions to their employees via voice mail rather than wait to give the directions in person. The problem with using voice mail in place of face-to-face communication is that it doesn't guarantee that the communication process takes place; the message sent may be received, but it may not be understood. Use of voice mail means that a sender is unable to judge by facial gestures or other body language whether the message has been understood and that the recipient(s) of the message is unable to ask questions when there is confusion. Mistakes can therefore easily occur when we send directions or other important messages via phone mail.

Maybe worse, many of those managers who are uncomfortable about communicating either one-on-one or with groups of their employees have begun to use voice mail as a crutch. It allows them to tell, instruct, lecture, or order, but since telling, instructing, lecturing, and ordering are not communicating (after all, true communication is a two-way process), it does not allow them to communicate.

E-Mail

Electronic mail should put an end entirely to telephone tag. We can send the detailed messages that don't belong on voice mail via e-mail and be assured that the parties to whom they are sent will receive them when they call up their e-mail. This is the plus of e-mail. Some software programs allow us to attach additional documents to our messages so that recipients get background information about an issue and can respond more knowledgeably to our message. Many people consider e-mail a godsend.

But not everyone uses it correctly. For instance, there are those who send e-mail messages just because they now have the technical capability to do so; it's like a child with a new toy. People who were compulsive memo writers continue to write— they've just found a new medium. And friends within our organization seem to think of e-mail as the equivalent of the notes we as kids passed across our desks while in school.

There is a skill to sending e-mail messages. Some managers' memos are indecipherable notes—phrases joined together with dashes—requiring a phone call to the sender for interpretation. Other messages ramble and are excessively long—the equivalent of several pages of paper. Writers of e-mail don't realize that electronic communications are still communications, and they don't take that extra moment to review and organize their thoughts before keying them onto the screen and pressing the Send button.

Often, too, senders of e-mail seem to assume that their recipients are mind readers or else are so familiar with everything happening within an organization that they can take a single sentence out of context and understand its relationship to the bigger picture. This isn't always so. A message like, "I told you Grant would approve the proposal" can be intriguing or confusing, depending on whether you know who Grant is and which proposal he approved.

I know a manager who often does this in conversations. We may be chatting about an assortment of issues; then suddenly she will say something like, "I took care of it, and I think it should work out well." Fortunately, standing beside her, I'm in a position to ask, "Which situation are you referring to?" A recipient of an ambiguous e-mail message might be embarrassed to respond, "Huh?" Message sent, message received, message not understood. Which means no communication took place.

There is also a preponderance of e-mail messages sent under the subject heading "FYI," which can make reviewing your morning e-mail messages frustrating, particularly if you receive many messages during the course of the day.

In today's organizations, communication isn't simply clarifying the nature and contents of your language; it is also a matter of improving the manner in which you relate to others. Which brings us to two other developments—the increasing interest in the differences in communication by gender and study of the patterns of communcation within teams.

Gender Communication

Publication of the book *Men Are From Mars, Women Are From Venus* by John Gray has increased interest in minimizing cross-talk between men and women. The book is designed to help men better understand women, and women better understand men. One way this can be done is by better understanding their communications, which has led to increased attention to gender as a communications filter.

To illustrate, writers on gender communication argue that women, as they grow up in our culture, are still taught not to be confrontational. As an example, when they ask questions, they are doing so instead of expressing direct opposition to an idea, a plan, or a proposal, as a way to make the other person rethink it. Men, on the other hand, aren't as aware of these indirect messages; when they ask a question, they want advice. Men also tend to be impatient with discussion of the details, preferring to get to the big picture and then move on, whereas women push for the details, in part to ensure that all issues have been addressed. Women also see conversations as a means of building rapport with others, as well as a way to explore another person's opinions, whereas men tend to see communication solely as a means for exchanging information or solving problems.

Publication of the book has triggered considerable discussion. Despite the popularity of the ideas, some people continue to debate whether there are gender differences in communication styles. Generalizing about any group or situation is troubling; it can be argued that introducing gender issues into the discussion has made effective communication seem more difficult, if not impossible, to achieve. On the other hand, interest in gender communication has probably made us more aware of other filters, such as cultural and language and perception problems, which I think is a good thing.

Meetings and Communication

The other major development is the study of teams and the communication that occurs within meetings.

In Chapter 7 I discuss meeting logistics. But while good judgment about when to hold a meeting means the end to unnecessary meetings and skill in management of meetings ensures productive use of meeting time, good interactions among participants mean a productive exchange of information. I would like to share with you some communication problems that occurred at a recent planning meeting in a southwest firm.

The product and marketing group had met to spend three days in planning. The eight members of the group had held operational meetings every Wednesday morning for three hours for the last two years. So the members should have been comfortable with one another. The only concern on their minds should have been the work left undone on their desks during the three-day meeting. Not so.

While Lois, the department head, was good at organizing meetings, she also had strong views on operating issues, which made it very difficult for her to listen with an open mind to opinions that differed from her own. She and her marketing manager, Marge, had worked together for some time, agreed on most subjects, and consequently controlled the discussions, leaving little opportunity for the other six members to contribute anything to the discussions. But then, as Arlene said to Sal prior to the meeting, "I'm sure it wouldn't matter if Lois didn't interrupt me all the time; she probably already has the plan for the year written up. Rather than waste these three days in meetings that aren't likely to reach any conclusions Lois doesn't want reached, I would be better off spending the time in my office coping with an overflowing in-box, not to mention lots of e-mail messages I have to return."

Sal nodded quietly. A relative newcomer to the department, just learning about the quick-mix baked goods line he oversaw, he had already come up against Lois and Marge, and his intention at this meeting was to maintain a low profile. He had had dinner with a former colleague from his old company, and the person had told him some exciting news about a new market study, but Sal was reluctant to talk about it even to the group. "I'll tell Hillary after the meeting," he thought. "We'll have made plans by then, but Hillary, as an old-timer with contacts throughout the organization, maybe can get the support outside the department to study this opportunity more thoroughly."

So the meeting began with two people firmly in charge and six others squirming in their seats. It didn't help, either, that Marge, in charge of the product division's sales and marketing, mentioned a brand-new ad campaign she had signed off on just the day before. "I wish I had known about it," Hillary said, a little put out. "I have a new dessert product that would have fit right in." "I thought I brought it up at an earlier marketing meeting," Marge replied. "I don't know if you were there, but you should have received the minutes." "Maybe," said Hillary, thinking, "Either I didn't check the minutes because I think those operating meetings are a waste of everyone's time—

dominated as they are by Lois and Marge—or I never got below the rest of the paper in my in-box to scan it."

The meeting continued.

The design department was there, and Lois reminded the group about the need to incorporate some new government regulations on one of the new cake-mix boxes. "We've taken care of that," Laverne said, quickly describing how the package design was going to be adapted to include the new two inches of required copy. Chris, startled, said, "I know we have to make these changes, but I hadn't really considered where we would put them. Maybe your idea would work, but it will play down how this mix can be used to prepare other desserts, which is a big selling point." As she spoke, Chris became increasingly upset about a decision being made about a product without her involvement.

Lois saw a potential conflict occurring—she had known about the change but hadn't thought to tell Chris, who had an explosive temper—so Lois quickly called a break. As she started toward the coffee machine, she said over her shoulder to Chris, "I gave Laverne approval to make the changes. I should have mentioned it to you, but you know how busy we've been lately in meetings. Take a look at the redesign. It's probably too late to make a change now, but we can certainly discuss it," she continued, coffee in hand, heading toward Marge. Chris stood perfectly still, trying to regain her composure.

Hillary came over to Chris, reminded her that blowing up at this meeting or any meeting with Lois would accomplish little, and Chris agreed, smiled wanly, and relaxed. But later that same day she again became upset when she learned to her surprise that a decision made at an earlier operating meeting had been reversed by Lois, and no one had known.

I don't think I have to tell you that the message that Lois and Marge were telling the rest of the "team" is that they couldn't care less what any one of the group's members thought or did. Lois and Marge considered themselves in charge, and everyone else was to do as told.

The group—I would never use the term "team" to describe these individuals working together—spent three uncomfortable days together. I can't say the end result was a very creative three-year plan, or that any new ground was broken. Certainly the group did not come up with any major money-making schemes. The final plan reflected pretty much more of the same, which was unfortunate, given the growing competition in the market for share. Sal kept his news to himself. Chris fussed and fumed throughout. Marge, in the catbird seat, smirked and smiled throughout as each and every one of her proposals was approved. Jeri, another newcomer, tried to get several new ways of marketing her product line approved, to no avail. "She'll learn," Hillary thought.

Clearly, this is a case of lots of talk—regular meetings, morning meetings every week, plus a three-day planning meeting—and not much communication. Lois hasn't learned the worth of stimulating participation by all the team's members or, more important, of listening to others' ideas and working as a team to come up with new and better ways of getting the work done or developing new products. She runs team meetings, and she does it well, but she has yet to gain the full advantages of a team, and she won't until she learns how to probe for ideas from her members, encourage feedback from other members, consider various options from different members, and, finally, develop action plans, where appropriate, based on group consensus.

The Balancing Act

If we're to improve both one-on-one and group communication, we need to utilize the communication and listening skills that have been taught over the decades. Similarly, our electronic communications can be clearer if we practice the same skills when we write electronically.

Improving communication can be accomplished by taking these steps:

• *Create an atmosphere of trust within the team setting.* Participants need to feel safe about sharing their ideas. They shouldn't worry that someone will kill off their idea with a negative word or embarrass them personally for their contribution—and that includes you. Don't become a Lois.

- *Encourage participation.* That means you have to get even participation; you don't want one or two vocal members to dominate the meeting. Unless it will make them uncomfortable, you may even want to call on those who you know have ideas but who tend to be quiet in the meeting. To do this, you may have to use your role as team leader to keep more outspoken members quiet. You might say, "I think you've got a number of great ideas. But I'd like to hear from some of our other members. How about you, Nancy?"

- *Use questions to control and guide the meeting, as well as to encourage greater input.* Let's say one of the team members is dominating the meeting—not you but Niles, the manufacturing manager. To take control of the meeting out of his hands, you might want to ask a direct question of another member on a topic related to what Niles was saying: "Henry, can you fill us in on how engineering is addressing the problems that Niles just mentioned?" Or if a member has been holding sway for some time on a team issue, you might ask, "Annie, what's your perspective on this issue? You worked in a company like our chief competitor's before coming here."

- *Don't answer questions raised at the meeting yourself.* In time, you'll find yourself doing all the talking and everyone agreeing with you—groupthink. You want to get others involved, which means relaying the question to another. For instance, you might say, "How would you answer Judy's question, Nellie?" Or, "That's an interesting question, Judy. How would you answer it?"

- *Defuse difficult or problem situations.* Maybe a member is going for a solution before the group has really addressed the problem. Or someone on the team is on your heels, challenging every word you say. Or a member of the team is on a shooting spree, killing everyone's idea. In the first instance, you might say to the person who is moving too fast, "I think we're moving too quickly. Let's make sure that we understand the nature of the problem before we get into what we should do, all right?" Rather than confront your challenger, ask the group to address his concerns. Ask the group as a whole, "What do you all think of Ned's objections to the approach we've agreed to?" The rest of your team is probably in agreement with your approach, but they won't say anything unless you ask.

If someone is challenging another member ruthlessly, you may want to talk to him during the break. Ask the individual to keep personalities out of the meeting or to hold back on his criticism of the other person's ideas for the good of the entire meeting.

For the person on a shooting spree, remind her that the objective initially is to get everyone's ideas on the floor: "We can evaluate what we have later."

- *Measure the quality of your communications with others.* Next time you meet with your employee, as you speak, note on a sheet of paper the number of times you interrupt him. Do the same at a team meeting. Or measure your level of communication dominance by noting how often the ideas come from you and how often you encourage others to speak.

- *Avoid always using voice mail and e-mail in place of face-to-face communication.* While there are savings in time in the use of the new technology, there is much that can be gained in person-to-person communications in being able to clarify misunderstandings or read body language to get real insights into what a person is thinking.

- *Be alert to the filters that can block your messages.* As managers in past decades were taught, be careful in your timing and choice of words (you don't want unnecessarily to create bad will between you and a staff member because of a poor choice of words). Don't let issues of education and language and technical background get in the way.

- *In talking to someone of the other gender, be sure that you are not cross-talking at each other.* For instance, Sarah might say, "Do you think we should enter into that agreement with the Glasgow organization?" Harold could respond, "I'm sensing that maybe you're not sure that a partnership with our Glasgow customer would make sense. Do you still have reservations?" Sarah: "Yes, I do. I think. . . ."

- *Learn which information you really need.* If there are reports you are getting that you don't truly need to do your job, call and ask that they no longer be sent. Likewise, think before sending a copy of a report or memoing a colleague on paper. Does she really need it?

- *Learn how to use e-mail correctly, starting with the message heading.* Be specific when composing your subject line. Compose your message headings so that both the nature of the message and the importance of the message are clear to the recipient.

- *Write effective e-mail messages.* Don't forget that e-mail messages are neither telegraphs nor novels. Rather, e-mail messages are short summaries intended to keep someone informed about progress or problems related to some situation.

When responding to someone else's e-mail message, you can save time for the recipient of your reply by eliminating that portion of the original message that is not relevant to your reply. That is possible with many e-mail programs.

- *Don't become a compulsive e-mail writer.* Ask yourself this two-part question: "Does this information need to be sent at all? What is the best way to pass it along?"

Regarding the first question, for a long time I found myself responding to messages to acknowledge receipt, a kind of rhetorical "Uh-huh, I agree," until I realized that each time I did so the person to whom I was replying had to call up and read the message. This was a waste of his time. So I stopped.

But there is a broader question here. When should you send any kind of communication—written or e-mail? You don't want to become a compulsive memo writer, no matter the format (paper or electronic). All you're doing is contributing to someone else's case of information overload. Any time you send a message to someone, ask yourself, "Does this message fall into the category of need-to-know or nice-to-know?" With nice-to-know information, you have to ask yourself how much it will be valued by the recipient. These are the same questions you should be asking yourself about paper correspondence.

- *Use the best format for communication.* On the issue of electronic transmissions versus paper, e-mail is best for those short updates on a problem or process. You shouldn't be sending lengthy memos or reports via e-mail. E-mailing a colleague who is also a friend a business message is one thing, even if you add a personal postscript, but you might not want to send birthday greetings for a forgotten birthday via e-mail.

• *To cope with your own information overload, begin to delegate responsibility for prioritizing your incoming communications.* Start by reviewing with your assistant or staff member those subjects that have greatest priority. Then go through your mail with the individual a few times to see if the person understands which materials get top priority and which go into your briefcase to be read during your daily commute or over the weekend.

Have this same individual clip or tag articles in trade or other business publications you receive that he believes you would like to read, judging from those priorities you agreed on. Your biggest responsibility is to keep this person informed of any changing information needs so that his judgment about which mail you are to see is accurate.

You'll also want to talk to your systems personnel to determine if there is some way your assistant or staff member can serve as intermediary for incoming and outgoing e-mail. Information that is not critical can be printed and left for you to see in that briefcase. Information that falls into the "must see" category can be sent on to your computer for reading first thing in the morning or right after lunch.

Have your assistant handle most incoming voice-mail messages, as well. Keep a separate phone number for critical messages, and share this number with only those individuals who need to speak directly with you or who might leave sensitive messages on your line. Otherwise, let all other calls go to your assistant, who can write down any messages for you to respond to when time permits. You save time not having to listen to each and every message and writing down return numbers and names.

7

Team Meetings: The When and the How

If the 1990s have brought a development that could be used either for good or for evil, it is teams and team meetings. There is considerable proof that teams made up of members from the same or different departments can be extremely productive, generating more and better ideas for new products and services, faster new product introductions, cost savings, better cycle time, and improved product quality.

Participation of employees in teams has also meant faster implementation of decisions and improved morale. Teams can pave the way for more and better quality ideas because they allow different experiences and perspectives to be drawn upon. That broader perspective also allows for a better analysis of any ideas the group comes up with and better choice of the final idea.

On the other hand, not all team initiatives have proven successful.

A high-tech company invested heavily in teams but saw no improvement in quality or productivity. Just the opposite. The problem seemed to be a lack of cultural change to go along with the organizational change. The organization's managers dominated, rather than facilitated, team discussions. And team members found themselves without the resources to put their ideas into practice; managers seemed unwilling to listen to their ideas. It didn't help, either, that the company continued to evaluate and reward employees on the basis of individual performance—no percentage of merit increases or bonuses was tied to team participation.

The involvement in the team efforts also meant that managers and employees alike did not have time to devote to their day-to-day activities, which created operational problems.

The Problem

The problem with teams appears to be fourfold: poor use of teams, poor meeting-management to ensure that time spent in meetings is efficiently used, poor efforts at bringing the team members together, and poor facilitation. (The last is discussed in Chapter 6 of this book.) This chapter addresses the logistical and cultural issues associated with teams.

Today, if you ask managers about teams, they complain about the amount of time participation in cross-functional teams or staff team meetings is taking up—and often with cause. Many admit they would not be at these meetings if they didn't think that senior management expected their involvement. Many of the issues that teams are being formed to deal with could just as easily be addressed via phone or e-mail.

Excessive amounts of time are also spent at meetings with a substantive purpose because team leaders don't know how to run meetings effectively. This results in time being taken away from day-to-day work, which can create operating problems.

Companies that have turned to teams to achieve the benefits from their use often don't realize what a high-maintenance approach teams are.

Team leaders and members need training in decision making and problem solving. Team leaders need training not only in meeting management but also in creating a culture of collaboration. In our enthusiasm for teams, we forget that not all people can work well together; teams aren't collaborative by nature—rather, teams are the means by which collaboration is to occur.

Many people think teams are a fad. After all, it seems as if their use skyrocketed, and many managers think they will soon fizzle out, replaced by another boardroom buzzword. While I believe they are being used excessively, I also believe that they are a method of management whose time has come. We may see fewer instances in which teams are used and fewer team meetings held as companies gain greater experience with them, but their application in solving problems or implementing ideas more quickly will continue because they fit right into the need for more collaborative workplaces.

Given the wave upon wave of downsizing in American business, the worth of each individual's contribution has grown—manager and employee. Team meetings may be less a matter of choice than of corporate survival, since they allow an organization to draw on the full creativity of its workforce. But if we're to maximize the potential of teams—whether self-directed work teams, cross-functional teams, or department teams—we must learn both the *when* and the *how* of team leadership.

Becoming Adept at Teaming

The When

Too often teams are used when the issue could just as well—or maybe better—be handled by an individual. Instead, managers and employees are assembled in a room to work together because of the approach's popularity, senior management's avid endorsement of the concept, and sometimes, sadly, a reluctance on the part of gun-shy managers to make a decision on their own (and suffer the consequences).

There is also a misunderstanding associated with team management. Too often physical teams—that is, groups of individuals that meet regularly to achieve results—are confused with the idea of "teamwork" or a sense of community that comes from shared objectives, such as a department's staff might have. Creating that kind of team has always been an important responsibility of department managers because it can increase group and individual job performance. Team meetings can contribute to this sense of teamwork, but they are only one of several ways to create a sense of belonging. Department managers who hold umpteen meetings monthly based solely on the assumption that such sessions will bring their staffs closer together are adding more to their employees' stress levels than to any sense of belonging—unless you count the communal feelings of frustration with their common manager.

Staff meetings can contribute to better communication, more and higher-quality ideas, and better decisions, but when are department meetings excessive? Similar concerns surround the creation of cross-functional teams. What benefits will be derived from having your peers work with you rather than communicate via e-mail or telephone? How about meeting for lunch for a one-on-one discussion? What would be the gain, in real terms, of assembling managers in a room to address a specific issue? Teams are great on a conceptual level, but they have to make sense on a practical level to justify the time commitment.

Right now, middle managers devote about two days a week to meetings (from problem solving to change management to product development to planning meetings). Senior executives spend as many as four days a week at meetings (discussing strategic and tactical issues as well as reviewing operational results). Furthermore, research suggests that both middle and senior executives can expect to spend about half a day more at meetings within the next few years. Unless we are more selective in deciding which situations demand group meetings and which don't, we could create a situation in which we spend so much time together in groups that we have no time to implement the decisions we make there. We may find ourselves having to outsource that responsibility!

The How

About 50 percent of team meetings are unproductive because they are mismanaged. There is an assortment of problems, from poor meeting preparation and lack of clearly defined missions or goals, to poor facilitation skills of meeting leaders, to lack of closure.

If you think that misused time doesn't cost, consider this statistic: An analysis of mismanaged meeting time at a mid-size Fortune 500 company, one with a reputation as one of the best-managed in America, disclosed wasted hours costing over $100 million annually spent on poorly run meetings. I mentioned that number to one trainer who specializes in team training, and she suggested that it understated the realities.

We may need also to convince some managers about the *why* or worth of teams, but that may become easier as we become more adept in using them.

WIIFM

Poor team leadership skills can mean a needless waste of time, team projects that aren't accomplished, and, maybe worst of all, continuation of the problems the team effort was to solve or loss of the creative idea that the team should have identified. Which can mean a poor department bottom line. Which can seriously affect your career.

Poor management of an operational meeting can erode staff productivity and destroy employee morale. You can even destroy the sense of team you work daily to create among staff. For instance, if you promise your staff input into decisions at group meetings but then are deaf to its suggestions, you can alienate staff to the point that it will not give you the commitment you need to achieve the department's mission.

A mismanaged cross-functional project in the past may make it almost impossible to bring peers together to work on a joint effort in the future.

The Idea That Almost Went Nowhere

Howard, a product manager with a hardware manufacturer, had an idea for a product extension for one of the product lines he oversaw. He needed help to produce a prototype, so he called the heads of manufacturing, marketing, sales, and customer service to see if these individuals would be willing to work with him on the idea. First, Howard called Karl, head of manufacturing.

"Karl," he said, "I know this idea will work, but I need you to produce some samples based on engineering's design."

"Do you have a design yet?" Karl asked.

"No," Howard replied. "But I'm sure Len in engineering will agree to join the team and work with us."

"Well," said Karl, "if he says yes, I'll join you, but only if Len agrees and is willing to take an active role in the team effort."

"OK," said Howard, disappointed. Everyone knew that Karl jumped at the chance to find less expensive ways to manufacture product, so his reaction to Howard's offer was a little disconcerting. Still, undaunted, Howard called Len. "After I get his agreement to work on the project, Karl will join up."

But Len was no more enthusiastic than Karl. "I understand your situation, Howard," Len said, "but I told you last year, after working on that last project with you, I wasn't going to be a puppet on one of your teams anymore. This idea sounds like it has potential, but I won't agree to be involved unless you promise to listen to members of the team and run your meetings better. Think about it, and give me a call."

Disheartened but still game, Howard next called Blanche, who headed up marketing. "I guess this idea might work, Howard, but I've been a part of new product idea teams you've led before. I've yet to see one of your ideas get tested, and quite honestly I can't waste my time on another idea of yours, whether it is a good one or not. I've got two unfilled positions in my department and haven't the time to determine if your proposal is another cockamamie idea or a moneymaker right now. If you have some information from potential customers that this idea might fly, send it to me. I'll make up my mind then."

Depressed, Howard called Susan, manager of customer service. Maybe she could come up with some way he could interest Karl, Len, and Blanche in the project.

"Hi, Howard, what's up?" Sue said. "Anything I can help you with today?"

Because of her warm greeting, Howard bared his soul to her and told her about the results of his three previous calls.

Sue's response: "Let's have lunch and talk about it."

Over their burgers and fries, Howard elaborated on his idea for a product extension that over time he believed could outsell the current product line. "But no one wants to get together with me on this," he whined. "It's a good idea, and they know it. Why don't they want to commit the time?"

"Howard," Sue replied, "you know the answer to that. The last team you led was a disaster. Remember, I was there, too. You had a good idea, a really good idea, but Len's, Karl's, and Blanche's ideas would have made it even better. But you wouldn't listen to anyone. You cut us off when we tried to talk, and you issued assignments as if we were your subordinates, not your peers. You lectured to us rather than treating us as collaborators who could bring our own experiences to the project and were willing to give up our work time to see this rough scheme of yours develop into a profit-making idea.

"No one came on time because no one wanted to be there—so meetings started later than scheduled," Susan continued, popping fries in her mouth as she spoke. "And your meetings usually ran longer than scheduled, too, because of your last-minute additions to the agenda. I don't want to hurt your feelings, but you know and I know that the final proposal, while it covered all the issues management expected us to address, was yours from first page to last. None of us felt we had contributed anything more than our names to the covering memo.

"Since we had reservations about the idea as you presented it, none of us was too disappointed when management turned the idea down."

"What can I do, Sue?" Howard wailed. "This idea I have now is really a good one."

"I think it is, too," Sue said, sighing. "So I'll help. But you've got to promise to help, too, by rethinking the way you manage your team sessions.

"We can get Blanche on board if we can convince her that the product idea has potential. So I'll call some distributors to get their feedback. You should call Len and apologize for the poor handling of the last team effort—maybe offer to rotate the chair of the project team, certainly agree to listen to member feedback during the course of the team project so that the sessions run more efficiently and effectively."

Thanks to Sue's input, Howard was able to assemble a team that included Karl, Len, Blanche, and several other managers and to produce a *group* proposal (Howard had learned his lesson), produce a prototype for testing, and manufacture and get his product on hardware store shelves quickly, before the competition. And, incidentally, Howard was right: It was a great idea, and the product extension that the group came up with did ultimately outsell the old line.

The Bottom Line

The moral should be clear: When you develop a reputation for mismanaging team meetings, you'll find it hard to get colleagues to be a part of teams you lead, no matter the reason for the team. Staff members have to tolerate the poor meetings of their supervisors or managers; they have no other choice. Not so your peers, unless they are forced to join up by some senior executive—and under those circumstances their contribution may be less than stellar.

Back to the Basics

In the past, the term "team" was used to refer to any department in which staff members worked collaboratively. Yesterday's "committees" and "task forces" come closer to the entities we now refer to as teams—groups of people representing different interests who meet for problem solving or decision making.

Meeting Experts

There is an old joke about camels being the product of committees. Meetings in earlier decades did not run any smoother than many of the team meetings we attend today. Although meeting-management was not a topic covered in business schools, companies valued those managers who knew how to run a meeting effectively. And judging by the quantity of management literature of the 1960s, 1970s, and 1980s on the topic, there were few such managers.

The literature of those years talks about the need for managers to:

• *Run meetings on schedule.* The meetings were to begin and end on time.

• *Prepare and distribute an agenda.* In general, the agenda was controlled by the chair, although members of the group could make recommendations.

• *Determine how decisions will be made.* Generally either the chair made the decisions using input from committee members or a vote was taken. The decision-making practices were discussed and resolved at the first committee meeting and became one of the operating rules the group adhered to.

• *Involve everyone in the discussion.* The chair wasn't to dominate the meeting or cut off members' remarks in mid-thought or allow participants to ramble on. The chair's responsibility was to stimulate participation by all members of the group.

• *Focus on issues, not personalities.* No one's comments were to be the target of a colleague's barbed responses.

• *Assign committee work.* Tasks were delegated and records kept of the due date when the tasks were to be completed, the nature of the work to be done, and the individual to whom the different assignments were made.

• *Write up meeting happenings.* A record was kept of all decisions made and actions taken during the session.

Those who might hold meetings were also advised about the *when* of meetings. There were two key questions managers asked themselves:

1. Do I need a meeting? Too often managers held meetings out of habit rather than when there was a need to exchange ideas and thinking; to gain group acceptance of an idea, program, or decision to increase the chances for its success; reach a group decision based on shared information; or reconcile conflicting views.

2. What are the meeting's objectives? It was drilled into the managers of earlier decades that there had to be a reason for a meeting, and its mission or goals needed to be identified when the memos inviting people to the meeting went out.

Team Spirit

Just as there were committees before teams, so there was an interest in a sense of team spirit. Interest in teamwork has existed since the 1920s. Research done as early as that showed that a feeling of belonging, coupled with greater involvement in decisions, positively affected employee output, quality, and other work dimensions. In the 1940s and 1950s, interest in teamwork and in employee involvement came together and led to employee suggestion systems and experiments in employee boards, maybe the first teams as we know them.

A review of the management literature of the 1960s, 1970s, and 1980s shows that the focus was very much still on creating a sense of teamwork within departments, however.

Developing a Group of People Into a Team

The earlier literature on teamwork advocated the following practices:

- *Help staff look at the department's responsibilities in terms of the corporation's survival.* When staff understands its department's role in the bigger picture, it is more motivated to pull together for the benefit of the organization.

- *Set short-term, medium-term, and long-term goals.* When employees set not only the mission but the strategic and tactical plans for the group, they appreciate their own importance to the organization—the relationship between their goals and the survival of the organization as a whole—and they work hard together to make the plans a reality.

- *Share responsibility.* Teamwork comes from shared responsibility not only in doing the work but in making the decisions about what work is to be done.

- *Have staff members support each other.* Managers organize the work to make the most of each member's contribution to the department, bringing staff members together so one member can help another. Over time, staff learns to rely on each other for help.

- *Have staff members keep each other apprised of their work.* When members are familiar with the work being done by co-members, they can step in to fill a member's place when he is away on vacation or on sick leave or just out to lunch.

- *Cross-train staff.* Cross-training allows staff members to fill in for each other when one is on vacation or on sick leave or to assist a coworker with a tight deadline or other kind of work crisis that demands a helping hand.

- *Manage on-the-job learning opportunities.* Members come together when they share knowledge. A manager's role is to determine what each person knows and to assign each member a buddy from whom she can learn new skills.

- *Acknowledge group accomplishments.* When staff can see the results of its efforts, it is encouraged to greater performance. Graphs on display can measure dollars earned, number of units produced, or survey responses from customers. Even negative numbers generate a strong sense of belonging—to work together to turn around the picture.

- *Encourage team initiative.* Managers who are good at developing a team attitude periodically hold problem-solving meetings at which their staff members can identify operating problems, prioritize them, and develop action plans to eliminate them.

  When their group accomplishes an action plan, they make it a reason for celebration.

- *Identify common language to foster cohesion and commitment.* A friend of mine tells me how her staff members all smile when she uses the word "pretty" to describe a well-designed ad page. It's a word that this account manager's team has learned to recognize as meaning "upbeat, smart, professional, appealing." Another manager I know can talk about "change overload," and her group knows that she's about to alert them to another new project it will have to complete. It's interesting that the phrase doesn't trigger anger; rather, it bonds the group together to think of ways of making the impossible possible.

- *Create a team identity.* It's not that managers good at creating a sense of teamwork have all their staff members running around in T-shirts with the department logo on it. But they do look for rites or ceremonies that will draw the group together. For instance, they might set aside half an hour every Monday morning for coffee and danish at which staff share with the group what they did the past weekend. It's a time for silliness and fun, not discussion about the workweek to come. Or they might put aside thirty minutes at the end of the week, on Fridays, just before everyone leaves, for gossip rather than talk about business—a time for department play. I know one manager who has some wound-up matchbox-size ducks, and he occasionally holds duck races with his staff on Fridays to help them rid themselves of the stress from the week that has just passed. Another manager makes a ritual of staying an hour after closing time on Friday for staff members with problems—business or personal—to come to chat.

And maybe T-shirts aren't such a bad idea, to help celebrate a special team accomplishment, like a T-shirt I still have and will always cherish from participating on a cross-functional team project.

- *Use humor.* Playful banter can relieve tension and make people comfortable wth one another, thereby supporting a team spirit.

- *Create team lore.* Stories about employees' persistence, creativity, and ingenuity can create an environment in which workers are encouraged to extend themselves and add new accomplishments to the department lore.

Fad Solutions

Today, teams—whether highly autonomous, self-directing groups of multifunctional professionals or employees—are the fastest-growing trend in American and European businesses. Aside from these self-directed groups, ever-increasing numbers of managers are holding department meetings to gain staff input into department initiatives.

It's possible to trace the beginning of teams to the late 1970s and 1980s, with the creation of quality circles (QC), when employees began to have a more active voice in solving operating problems and addressing other managerial issues.

Initially the goal of the QCs was to increase quality control using statistical analyses conducted by the employees, but over time these QCs' purpose grew to include a wide range of issues that affected work and employee satisfaction. Task teams or project teams of employees were formed to cope with problems beyond product quality or service. Some of these groups were led by management, and others operated without supervisory or managerial direction. Employees joined their supervisor for planning sessions to contribute their input in action plans. By the 1990s, when U.S. companies' serious romance with teams began, supervisors had some understanding of what it took to create a sense of teamwork within a work group and how to run an effective meeting. The problem today is that many managers have yet to blend both competencies to help create the kind of meetings in which individuals can join together to fully utilize their experiences and perspectives to solve problems or make decisions.

Team-Based Pay

Another problem contributing to difficulties in creating effective teams is a lack of recognition for team contribution.

A study by Hay Associates (a consultancy) showed a relationship between poor team performance and lack of team-based pay. There is not yet a means of fairly compensating team participation. While there are a number of interesting efforts in this regard, they are all at the experimental level. If companies with great dependence on teams wait too long, Steven E. Gross, a Hay vice president and author of the book *Compensation for Teams* (New York: AMACOM, 1995) says, they run the risk of erasing all the progress they've made toward building successful teams. The Hay study found that the dominant means of compensating team efforts in 1996 was recognition awards (noncash and spot cash) from a team award pool. The size of the team pool was determined by productivity, customer satisfaction, financial performance, and product quality; the awards themselves were divided among members, with each member receiving an equal amount.

The problem with team-based pay remains unchanged: the difficulty of assessing each individual's contribution to the team. To date, reviews involve evaluations from peers, managers, and customers, including the 360-degree reviews, but evaluations from superiors still carry the most weight in any appraisal of performance. Companies still have reservations about the ability of team members to conduct objective assessments of those within the group—and conversations with team participants suggest they have cause for concern. Long-term rivalries, turf issues, personality conflicts, and the like, they say, can influence peer evaluations. And so long as there is concern among team members that they won't get a fair rating from their peers, a problem with team evaluations exists.

The Balancing Act

In an earlier book, *The High-Value Manager*, my coauthor, Randi T. Sachs, and I wrote about the competencies—skills, abilities, and knowledge—critical to successful team management. In retrospect, it is evident that those competencies reflect good meeting-management skills and the ability to create within the team a sense of common purpose or belonging. For team efforts to produce outstanding results, we need to apply to them the best we have learned from the past about running effective meetings and creating a team spirit.

You need to:

• *Remember that it's the team's meeting.* As meeting managers of past committees learned, you have to have an agenda for your meeting. But as today's team leaders, you develop that agenda with your team. You may be the team leader, according to the group's sponsor or because of job title, but the team should determine what will be discussed and when and where the group will meet.

You'll want to handle logistical issues in ground rules set on the first day. For instance, you may want to suggest to the team that you rotate the chair in a self-directed work team or cross-functional team. And, to make clear to the group that you support conceptually the idea of a team effort, seat yourself anywhere but at the head of the table—that's the traditional position of authority, and taking it could send a negative message to your team members about how you view the operation of a team.

To ensure that the meeting starts and ends on time, you might want to project a visual of the agenda as an effective reminder to all present of the time limitations. Thus, you share the burden with your staff or project team of keeping the meeting moving forward.

• *Determine how decisions will be made.* This is another operating principle that you should cover at the first meeting. As those who ran meetings in the 1960s, 1970s, and 1980s soon learned, failure to delineate how issues will be addressed can create conflicts following deliberations.

If you promise to share decision making with the team, be sure you keep the promise. Too often, after making just such a promise, leaders violate the promise by making a decision by fiat. This can unite the team, yes, but against you, for violating the team's trust.

Don't think I am advocating that all decisions within a team environment be consensus-based. Just the opposite. The decision-making approach should be appropriate to each decision. In cross-functional teams, for example, decision making usually can be shared with the team. In department meetings, on the other hand, you can reserve the right to make some decisions by fiat while sharing other decisions with the group. You might say, "I will want your input on all the issues we discuss, but there may be some that I will have to make the final decisions on. I promise, however, to hear you out. And if my final decision differs from the group's, I will explain to you, whenever I can, the reasons for this."

• *Clarify objectives and address any confusions about the team's mission.* Department managers learned how clear direction created a sense of teamwork within their staff that contributed to the department's success in achieving its bottom line.

Today's teams fail when their members don't know what

they're supposed to do or when what they are supposed to do makes no sense within the big picture. Your task as team leader is to make clear to the group the reason it has been created—its place in the big picture.

Toward that, you'll want to work with your team members to answer these questions:

1. What is the exact objective of the team? (Plan to revisit this objective periodically to see if it has changed; circumstances may require a rewording of the group's mission.)
2. Do action plans exist to meet the goals?
3. How much latitude does the team have to achieve its mission? To what extent will the team have to get approval from the group's sponsor?
4. What are senior management's expectations about the team's outcomes?
5. Is the goal or mission of the team realistic in light of the resources it will have access to?
6. If the resources the team needs are not forthcoming, how much flexibility does the team have to rewrite its charter or mission to reflect the realities?

Answering these questions as a team not only prepares the members for the effort to come but unites the group around a common understanding about the obstacles it may have to overcome to complete the project in a manner that will constitute successful completion in the opinion of the sponsor or senior management. Again, you create a team spirit that strengthens the group's resolve to work together to achieve its objective.

It may help you to achieve your objective by setting short-term goals for the team—stages to complete until the team achieves its mission. Again, another lesson from the past: Start with small goals whose success keeps enthusiasm high.

• *Ensure team training.* You should consider training in facilitation skills for yourself and have team members trained in decision making, critical thinking (both analytical and creative thinking), and interpersonal skills for your team to ensure good interactions among members and achievement of the team's stated outcomes.

In the committee meetings of the past, Robert's Rules of Order were all members needed. The chair was in charge. Today, in contrast, the team leader shares control of the meeting with the other members. And training in interpersonal skills ensures member support in encouraging participation of all the team's members. And it makes reaching consensus on decisions a whole lot easier.

• *Remember that you don't have all the answers.* Otherwise, why would you have assembled others to get their input? This guideline is as applicable in running operating meetings whose purpose is to develop a sense of teamwork within the staff as in cross-functional group meetings where you want to encourage collaboration among the members.

It was something the chairs of yesteryear's committees kept in mind, and it is doubly critical to remember in today's team sessions.

• *Don't pass judgment or comment on members' remarks and ideas.* Whether you're at an operational meeting or on a cross-functional project, acting like an expert or a critic will destroy team spirit and inhibit discussion. Even if you have reserved the right to make the final decision, your promise was to hear all views out before making that decision.

Good meeting management calls for you to stimulate participation from all members, and you won't get this if your team members—particularly those more shy members—feel that their comments will be the target of attacks by you or another team member. (For more on stimulating communication, see Chapter 6.)

• *Counter groupthink.* You want to generate a team spirit as the managers in past decades were urged to do, but you don't want to do so at the cost of a good decision.

If you're to get the benefits of different perspectives and experiences, you need to learn to commend those who disagree with the majority, even if you're a part of that majority. You can do that by asking group members what faults they see in the idea everyone loves, or you can play devil's advocate, raising questions that should be raised but aren't being raised due to groupthink. Or, if the team's members tend to agree with everything you say, learn to hold your opinion until discussion is concluded.

• *Listen empathically*. Members shouldn't have to worry that you will use your position to cut them off or put down their remarks. Remember the lessons taught meeting managers in the past.

Members of your team should feel free to voice their opinion, even if they know that it is contrary to yours. They shouldn't be placed in the position of one manager who was interrupted by her boss as she was voicing her opinion. She stopped in midsentence, then continued, "Oops, forget it. If I continue, I'm in for a lecture."

• *Share control of the meeting*. Let me remind you again: It doesn't matter if someone in senior management asked you to form a group to address the issue or if it was your idea to form a team to examine an operating problem or fine-tune a new product idea you came up with, à la Howard. That doesn't mean you control the discussion. Your role is to facilitate discussion. Your objective is like that of department managers in the past: to make members of the group into a team.

• *Create a sense of camaraderie among team members*. I'm talking about developing that team spirit that managers in the 1960s, 1970s, and 1980s were exhorted to develop within their departments. That might entail remembering a member's birthday and celebrating it as a part of the team meeting or acknowledging a member's persistence in obtaining critical information for the team by telling of the member's efforts in all its detail, a story that in time becomes both team lore and a standard other members will have to meet. Maybe provide chocolate chip cookies, if that's your style, so members with a sweet tooth look forward to the meeting, or have pens made on which the team's goal is printed. Or, as one team I know did, come up with a jazzy name for the project you're working on, like the Genesis Project for an effort that the members believe will be a new way of working together, or the Godzilla Manual to reflect the breadth of the effort, or the Mash Unit, which could reflect the seriousness of the endeavor or, in jest, the group's addiction to old *M*A*S*H* reruns.

• *Handle meeting logistics.* As team leader you don't direct the discussion, but as leader you are responsible for the drudge work. Sorry, but the position makes you responsible for reserving a meeting room, seeing that the agenda is distributed, gathering and distributing relevant documentation ahead of the meeting, and checking out any audiovisual or telephone hookups (if you have off-site members) to see that everything works as it should.

As team leader, you are responsible for the planning and execution of the meeting, which includes the organization of seats to facilitate discussion. So you'll want a round or rectangular table rather than a lecture-style seating arrangement.

You also need to address problems with lack of resources. It's primarily your responsibility to get the resources the team needs to achieve its charter. You'll have to talk to those with access to these resources (either the team's managerial sponsor or other members of management) or partner with other teams to share resources.

Identify those members of the team who tend to support others on the team and those others who influence the team in a negative way. Be prepared to divert discussion when personality issues take control over objective assessment of ideas.

• *Provide praise and positive feedback to team members.* Letting members know that their effort is appreciated encourages them to continue to contribute at a high level to the team. The value of praise has been extolled in almost every management text, but praise continues to be rarely given when deserved, even in traditional manager-employee relationships, let alone in team sessions.

• *Support team-based pay initiatives.* As the stakes from successful team initiatives get higher, so must the recognition to team members for a job well done. A pat on the back, free lunch or dinner for two, even a celebratory dinner for the team members is not sufficient reward for a team that potentially could save a company several thousand dollars or make it hundreds of thousands, even millions of dollars. That means team-based pay plans that recognize both the team as a whole and any outstanding efforts by one or more members. Studies into the best way to do this are still under way; your role is to support your own organization's efforts to test rewards programs.

In my opinion, the best team-based pay plans may be those based on an assessment by members of each participant's contribution to the team effort, using specific criteria set by the group at the start of the team effort. In essence, the standards by which member participation is measured constitute another operating rule set by the team members themselves. Of course, all team participants—managers and employees alike—would have to undergo training in both selecting criteria for evaluation and conducting objective evaluations in a team setting.

• *Provide closure.* Members should leave with a feeling that the time spent at the meeting was well spent. Review with the group the decisions reached. Summarize who is responsible for what, when it has to be done, and which topics will be carried forward to the next meeting.

• *Celebrate team accomplishments.* Acknowledge individual achievements as well as group accomplishments. And use these wins to generate further achievements.

• *Keep a record of decisions reached.* This is often a problem with meetings today. No record is kept. As a result, members of one cross-functional team often query each other a few days later about who said what and what final decision was reached. Making minute-taking a regular part of the meeting logistics solved the problem. Responsibility for taking minutes is rotated among members. And, needless to say, the objective is to get them in the hands of meeting participants as soon as possible.

8

Value-Driven Organizations: Differences Between Values and Norms

Employees need values to work toward and to help them direct their actions. Values are especially important in organizations where employees have been empowered to make decisions on their own. Values unite employees under common goals, without the need for corporate rules and regulations and an organization hierarchy.

Even in more traditional companies, employees no longer want to obey orders mindlessly. They want to know "why." Values answer that question.

Values are developed by top management from the company's marketing strategy and have objectives like the following:

The best value for customers' money in each and every product sold.

Work smarter, not harder.

Products and services that satisfy internal and external customer needs.

Open and honest communication with each other.

An opportunity for each employee to reach her highest potential.

Intelligent risk taking to ensure corporate viability and renewal.

Teamwork from winning teams.

Empowered employees who excel.

Two-way communication.

A diverse workforce.

Mutual respect and sincere concern about others' needs.

Personal growth opportunities for employees—greater employability.

Recognition and reward for excellence and outstanding performance.

Shared responsibility for the company's profitability.

The impact on corporate performance of practicing these
values should be self-evident: satisfied customers; an organization that is always renewing itself; empowered employees; high
productivity; mutual trust and self-respect—all factors critical to
corporate competitiveness.

The Problem

Unfortunately, in many companies that have adopted value sets,
there are gaps between the values promulgated by managers
and the values they practice—that is, the informal rules by
which the company operates. The organization is not walking
the walk. And where that's the case, confusion reigns. When
nothing is done to align the values promulgated with management actions, morale declines and productivity plummets.

Values have a real purpose, so they aren't something that we
can expect to disappear from the business scene. But the current
problems with them will have to be solved.

We need to close the gap between the values preached by
management to employees and the norms practiced by the same
management, particularly since the values promulgated by management are positive, whereas the norms practiced by managers
are generally negative.

Too often corporate values do not reflect the managerial realities—and employees know it. Maybe more important, follow-

ing the publicizing of the value sets, employees see no efforts made by managers to change workplace norms so that they are in sync with the corporate values. There is no change in the behavior of either senior management or lower-level managers to suggest that either is serious about making the values a reality. Yet employees are bombarded with questions about what they are doing to make the values a reality.

The Value Gaps

Remember the old axiom "Do what I say, not what I do"? That appears to reflect management's attitude about the value system.

"Mistakes are learning experiences." So why does someone whose new product failed suddenly get demoted? "Customers' needs are our first priority—internal and external." So why does Steve, who is known for never returning customers' calls, get a promotion? Why does Jeff, who snaps at his department's internal customers when they suggest that their department and his get together to smooth out workflow, get an award for his "cooperative efforts"? If "Management does not accept mediocre performance," why does Alice's supervisor allow her to stroll into the office cavalierly after 9:30 when she's due in at 9 A.M. like the rest of the staff?

Here are other examples employees tell me about:

• Senior management sets honesty as a value, but company norms turn a blind eye to discrepancies in travel and expense vouchers under 15 percent.

• Management sets on-schedule delivery as a value, yet managers cavalierly chat on the phone or with one another while a critical shipment is kept on hold.

• In its desire for new revenue sources, management advocates that employees "think outside the box," yet when an employee identifies a company that might ally with his company to produce a new product with the potential for big sales, the worker gets slammed by his supervisor for not giving his full attention to his daily work.

What do these situations say to the employees about these managements' advocacy of the values of honesty, on-schedule delivery, and out-of-the-box thinking to generate new revenue streams? The message: The values are meaningless. Management credibility, suffering already from corporate statements like "our people are our most important assets" followed by wave after wave of downsizing, sinks to a new low.

Fear Management

The worst situations occur over values tied to people's worth, mutual respect, and empowerment in organizations where nothing is done about those managers who manipulate and bully employees and otherwise mistreat them on the assumption that fear will prod them to higher levels of performance.

Let's say that the company's people values are to "build a sense of teamwork," "create a climate of risk taking," and "demonstrate an appreciation of the work of each and every employee," yet you work for a manager who, after a wave of layoffs, said within your hearing, "I think it motivates employees to come to work with fear in their bellies." He does not recognize employees for outstanding work—he's actually told his staff that he hasn't the time to acknowledge their performance; he dominates team meetings, interrupting employees; he takes credit for his staff's ideas; and while he speaks fluently about the worth from empowering employees, he pounces on any employee who makes a decision without first checking with him.

If you worked for this manager, how seriously would you take the people values promulgated by your company?

Let's look at two other value sets: customer satisfaction and corporate profitability. Imagine you think you know how you could influence both, yet your boss says no, without explanation, to your idea. That's what happened to Lynn.

Lynn is a customer service rep who works for a southern retail chain. Concerned about the decline in the company's customer index, she proposed to Mel, her boss, that the customer service department conduct a survey to determine those actions the chain could take to change the downward direction the index was taking. But each time she raised the issue, Mel rejected her suggestion. Pressed for an explanation, he brought up the budget. "Now isn't the time to ask management for the money. Maybe when times are more prosperous," he told her. Yet, in Lynn's opinion, the store won't experience more prosperous times until management finds out why customers have started to go to the competitors instead of to her company's stores.

Corporate Mixed Messages

Sometimes the problem is on a corporate level. The organization creates the value statements but falls short in demonstrating its commitment to them. One example: One company I know has the value "to increase employee growth and advancement." Last year that company cut its training budget and discontinued its policy of reimbursing tuition for employees who study evenings to earn degrees. The decision wasn't prompted by a bad year; the company is having one of its best years ever.

There's still another problem with values as they are often used by companies. Often the values are so broad that employees have no idea how the value translates into behaviors or practices or impacts their current job responsibilities. Consequently, the values don't help the employees with their day-to-day work. Employees have their own workplace norms, and it is these that influence their behavior, even when they are in conflict with the values promulgated from top-down.

Generally, employee norms are answers to questions about what kind of performance can get them promoted, which rules can be broken and which rules can only be bent, and how they can impress their bosses without breaking into a sweat. It's the answers to these questions that provide employees with direction, not the values set by management. Let's take one major company that has as its goal to become a global organization over the next five years. Toward that end, one of the values set by the organization is to "Think global." Which is fine—except that most of the employees have no idea how that value reflects their own job. Their management has promulgated the value, along with five others (respect for the individual, customers first, dedication to quality, better customer relations, a willingness to take reasonable risk), but it hasn't translated this one—or, for that matter, the other five—into behaviors that employees should practice. Consequently, the value set, while important to the company's mission and strategy, means little or nothing to the workforce, so it is doing nothing to help make that objective a reality.

WIIFM

"I don't set the values," you argue. "I'm a middle manager [or a supervisor], and I just have to communicate them to my employees."

But as a middle manager or supervisor, you are in a critical position to see that the values are practiced. Why should you do that? If you don't, the productivity and morale in your department, maybe already in trouble from previous downsizings or restructurings, could decline further. Your employees want a reason to believe in their organization, and the value system is not it when they perceive a clear gap between what is being promoted and what is the reality of the workplace. What they want are values and norms that are credible as evidenced by the fact that they are truly being practiced by those above them in the corporate hierarachy. It's your job to see that this happens and that your employees have clear direction about how they can practice them, too.

Certainly, if your norms are contrary to the value set, it is your responsibility to begin to adapt your own behavior to reflect the cultural shift.

Back to the Basics

We have always had workplace values of one sort or another that influence employee behavior. It's only since the 1980s that values have become linked to corporate performance.

Employee Norms

Employee norms are informal values, and they have probably been around since Cro-Magnon man. Grog turned to Ugh, pointed to the sun going down, and both headed home. They would figure out how to roll that stone when the sun came out the next day.

Within a few weeks in a job, new employees usually know what a company's norms or informal rules are, and they practice them, or find themselves ostracized by their peers or in trouble with their bosses. Some of these norms have to do with the social side of the organization, such as which employees you can safely confide in and which you can't and whom you can lunch with and whom you can't given your position, and others reflect the way the work is done—which secretary has the right to cut in front of everyone else to copy something at the copier, who on staff can be counted on to share office supplies and who can't, and what is considered hard work, punctuality, early departure, and the like.

The earliest recorded norm was probably the "work ethic." If you arrived late or left early or took more than an hour for lunch, you were said to lack the "work ethic." *Webster's Dictionary* defines "work ethic" as "a belief in work as a moral good." At most companies, it simply means you are a hard worker. Poor performers are said to lack the "work ethic." McGregor's Theory X managers assume that all employees lack a work ethic unless proven otherwise, whereas his more participative Theory Y managers think most people have a strong work ethic and just need the opportunity to prove it. Conscientious, industrious, committed to work, and motivated—all are adjectives that are used to describe those who possess the work ethic. The qualities may be important to an employee's achieving her job goals, but goals have never really been tied to the work ethic. And goal setting may be what we need to consider to find solutions to the problems currently being encountered with values.

Goal Setting

Goal setting makes sense, since values are goals that the organization has set for employees to ensure its achievement of its strategy.

Goals are the end products of the planning process. Planning is only the means of achieving them. The process is usually top-down. The company has overall goals that establish the direction for each of its divisions. These divisions, in turn, have goals that determine the plans of the work groups within them. For instance, a corporate goal might be to increase production by 20 percent within a year. The division might determine that it will have to reduce downtime caused by equipment trouble, improve operating procedures, and upgrade skills. Your group, in turn, might decide that to achieve the division's goals and thereby the corporation's goals, your employees will each have to learn how to troubleshoot equipment problems by mid-year, conduct a study of materials deliveries, and complete cross-training so that there will be a backup crew member for each process.

To come up with those ideas, you and your team:

• Considered the goals of the organization as a whole and the needs of its internal and external customers.

• Analyzed how department strengths would help and department weaknesses would hinder the group's ability to meet the needs of the organization as a whole and its external or internal customers.

• Identified opportunities to make a greater contribution to the company's goals or strategy. Part of this process was to look into the future to see how circumstances would impact your operation, positively and negatively.

Of course, you can't predict with certainty what will happen. No one expects that. But you can make very good assumptions on the basis of what you know about the past and the present. So your forecasting task requires that you consider the plans not only of your own management but of competitors, customers, suppliers, maybe even the government if it could affect your company's future.

• Identify goals for the department that will contribute to the company's goals and that are attainable by the department, considering its strengths and weaknesses.

Managers new to planning quickly learn not to create a laundry list of goals that, while they might make it look like the three or four days in planning were well spent, are impossible to meet. You and your team should come up with three or four meaningful goals that are likely to be achieved during the time-frame of the action plan.

• Prioritize the goals. You make judgments about how to allocate funds and staff effort to ensure that the most important goals are met, then the next important, and so on.

The goals are the targets for the department for the next quarter, year, or the next three years, and each one set:

1. Is specific. Everyone knows what the desired result is, so there is a good likelihood of its being achieved.
2. Is behavior- or performance-based. Employees know what actions they must take to contribute to the goal being met.
3. Is realistic. When a goal isn't reachable, it lacks meaning, and employees burn out from the frustration of trying to achieve this. I'm not just talking here about the skills or ability or motivation of employees; I'm talking about the corporate realities as well. If you set a goal that you know is in conflict with corporate procedures or that demands an outlay of dollars during a tight economic period, you have to be prepared to fight the uphill battle with senior management to change those norms or get that budget allocation to support your employees' efforts.
4. Is observable or measurable. If not, it's impossible to know if or how well the goal is being met. This monitoring process, in turn, ties the goals to performance evaluations. Employees and the manager agree on the goals (or key results or outcomes) that the employee is to achieve for the year to support department, division, and corporate goals.

Management by Objectives

Management by Objectives (MBO) was the system most in use by companies in the 1980s, when interest in values first developed. Its popularity stemmed from evidence that it could ensure results. Manager and employee would meet to establish the objectives that the employee would accomplish over a given time, usually a year. These were written down, and both the manager and employee had a copy. At regular intervals, the two would get together to review the employee's performance and establish new objectives or modify old ones in light of changing circumstances. The results could be some units on a scale or dollar figure, but they also could be a desired attribute or condition that was important to the organization.

Critical to the success of MBO was communication—of the standard, of the employee's progress in achieving that standard, and of the final review at year's end.

MBO still exists in many companies, but it is only one of a number of systems currently being used to evaluate employee performance. Whether the objective is called a goal, a key result, or an outcome, whether the employee is assessed quarterly or twice a year, and whether the employee and manager conduct the assessment together or independently and then review each one's conclusions, the concepts pretty much remain the same.

With some adaptation, this same process can be applied to values.

Fad Solutions

Interest in values can be traced as far back as the 1950s, when researchers into organizational psychology looked into what made successful companies and came up with informal organizational elements. Writing in *Personnel Journal* in April 1986, William J. Corbett called it "an amorphous 'feeling in the air.' " Researchers in the 1960s talked about the business "climate." But managements didn't really become interested in this "feeling in the air"—this thing called "climate"—until the downturns of the 1970s and 1980s. They prompted them to study for themselves the elements in the air that seemed to make a difference in corporate performance.

This represented a major shift in strategy. Until that time, companies had looked at developing technologies and marketing schemes and organizational shifts within their small business units (SBUs) to achieve competitive advantage. But in the 1980s, managements took another approach, focusing on changing the ways people behave to improve corporate performance. The same research methodology and models that had been used to study the cultures of the past were applied to existing corporate cultures, which meant corporate rites and rituals (like the Friday afternoon beer parties in Route 128 companies outside Boston), development of hero stories (like those about Bill Marriott made famous by the Peters/Waterman book *In Search of Excellence*), and corporate values and norms.

By the 1990s, "values" had become a buzzword, along with another "v" word—"vision"—and cause. Values grow out of corporate vision.

The initial values that came from the models were so similar that they could have been reproduced on a copier machine. They included such values as "Make money," "Treat people as valuable assets," and, my personal favorite (which almost every company adopted at the time), "Have fun." These values came closer to maxims about motherhood and apple pie than guidelines for achieving corporate strategy. All these corporate values came into this editor's office on laminated cards that were distributed to employees to help them remember the values that should direct their actions.

It seemed as if values were just another management fad based on the management literature of the time, but that was almost ten years ago. Those companies that created values that reflected real-world market needs proved that they could energize a corporation. The problem facing companies today has more to do with the means by which companies try to get employee buy-in than with the value systems themselves.

Employee Input

Values generally come from senior management, although they can also be created for a department to help it redirect employee efforts toward its mission or strategies. When top management develops the values, the first time employees hear about them is in a memo or at a corporate staff meeting. Here's the problem: Employees are promised input into the values, and staff meetings are held in which employees devote considerable thought to them, but generally these meetings make very little difference.

The biggest problem is the discrepancies between the values and the real way the business operates. Neither the values nor the organization is changed to put the values and norms in sync. Employees at best are confused and at worst are demoralized, as they see the promised opportunity to have a voice in the values lead to naught.

The more often these meetings are held with little change in either the values or work environment to get them in sync, the more frustrated employees get about the whole thing.

Values and Job Evaluations

Seeing little change in the values is bad enough, but problems really develop when companies attempt to tie their newly developed values to job evaluations without first translating those values into behaviors or activities that employees can use to guide their actions.

Let me give you a simple example. Your company has as a value "to satisfy customers." Paul, a facilities worker at one of the company's branches, sees a piece of wastepaper on the floor and walks by without picking it up. You see him and call him into your office.

"Paul, why didn't you pick up that paper on the floor?"

"I guess I wasn't thinking," he tells you.

"But, Paul," you say, "it's critical that our facilities look spotless. That's important if we're to 'satisfy our customers.' Don't you realize you violated an important corporate value back there?"

"Huh?" Paul responds. "You've got to be kidding. I admit there could have been an accident, but what do those values have to do with a single sheet of paper on the floor?"

"It's a matter of corporate image," you proceed to explain. Paul is willing to listen to your explanation and to promise to be more observant in the future. This means the problem shouldn't recur. But the situation would never have occurred in the first place if you had explained to him what the value "to satisfy customers" meant to his job.

The Balancing Act

We can solve many of the problems associated with values by applying the know-how we have developed over the years in departmental and employee goal setting. Values are attributes, and employees can be measured in their efforts to achieve values if you and they together identify behaviors and practices they must follow, as well as examine their job to identify how specific responsibilities impact the values.

Goals aren't reached when they aren't clearly defined or are too general or when those who are responsible for achieving the goals don't know why they should achieve them, think something is more important to be achieved, or don't know how to achieve them. They also aren't achieved when we set goals for our department and employees with our employees, yet don't practice the same behavior we expect of our employees or support them by our actions. This also holds true for values.

We can learn much about how to make values a compass to direct employee activities by keeping in mind the basics of good goal setting. These include the following points:

• *Employees need to know why the values are important.* That's as important for values as for goals. Employees who have no idea of the importance of goals don't work hard to achieve them. Your employees won't be concerned about the values set by their company unless you explain why they are critical to the company's competitive advantage. They likely won't care until you explain to them how they are tied to the company's competitive position or market strategy.

Too often, values are promulgated by senior management, but the reasons behind the values don't get down below the managerial ranks. Your employees won't know those reasons unless you tell them.

• *Employees need to know how to translate the values into job performance.* Employees need to relate the goals and values to their responsibilities and how their work can influence their achievement. Telling your employees about a value means nothing unless it is translated into activities or behaviors they can follow. Think about Paul. If he knew that he needed to keep the walking areas clean of trash and help the branch set an example of orderliness and organization, he would not have thought twice about picking up the litter on the floor.

• *Employees have to have their priorities straight.* Unless you make clear which activities are tied to important goals and thus have greater priority, those activities may not be done first. The same applies to values and the behaviors tied to them. If an employee knows how critical it is for him to collaborate with colleagues to get a new product off the drawing board, because that's the behavior tied to the company's values to "practice healthy dissatisfaction with the status quo" and to "collaborate for renewal and continued growth," the employee will find the time to participate in that team effort.

Here's when it is important that employees get a single message. There should be no confusion from managers who say one thing and practice another or from job requirements that conflict with the values.

One buyer experienced this kind of confusion. His plant set as a value "practice just-in-time (J-I-T) inventorying," yet a key part of his job was to ensure that supplies were on hand to prevent manufacturing downtime. The employee chose to purchase more supplies than the J-I-T system demanded because the production manager yelled when there was machine downtime. His boss explained the values but did not support the employee by helping him find some way to satisfy both requirements.

• *There need to be positive consequences for employees who pursue the values.* When employees meet their goals or achieve the key results set with you, you give them a raise, maybe even a bonus, depending on the goal's difficulty. Those who demonstrate their support of corporate values also need acknowledgment. It doesn't have to be a cash bonus. It can be lunch for two or a plaque, but it should tell the employee "you did well."

Presenting the award also gives you an opportunity to reinforce the importance of the value, the behaviors or practices associated with the value, and the roles and responsibilities of employees to see that the value is achieved.

• *Employees should not be allowed to think they are practicing the value when they actually aren't.* Goals aren't met when employees aren't clear about what they need to do to achieve them. So it is with values. Failure to translate values into activities can cause similar confusion.

• *They should not see others being rewarded for not practicing the value.* Which can happen in the case of values if employees see that their managers are not criticized for their failure to support the values. Remember the manager who failed to collaborate with other team leaders yet received an award for being cooperative?

Implementing a Department Value System

If you decide to implement a values system on a departmental level, given the higher productivity associated with its application, you need to think through your approach. Just as employees need to be truly involved in goal setting for them to buy into those goals, so your employees need to be involved in identifying the values important to your department's mission, identifying the norms, determining where conflicts exist, and developing solutions to align values and norms.

You also need to demonstrate your commitment to achievement of the values by your words and deeds. If Howard, head of human resources, truly wants to support a diverse workforce, then he should support the internship program suggested by Gail, his assistant, which would prepare minority members for managerial positions. And if Dick, a product manager, wants his team to come up with a new product offering, then he needs to free his staff from its day-to-day work for a few weeks to allow it to research several ideas it has on the drawing board even if it means that he has to pay for some high-priced temps over that period.

Begin by asking your employees each to write on a sheet of

paper five factors they consider critical to achieving the department's mission or goals for the year. You can do this as a part of the department's planning process.

Examine the results, and place on the board those thoughts that most closely resemble one another. Now have the group vote on the five values they think are most important to achievement of your department's mission.

The five chosen should be clearly defined for everyone. At least, you should define the terms of any value statements you decide on. For example, what do you mean by product quality? Customer satisfaction? Teamwork? You and your employees should be clear about what you're trying to attain or what value judgment is driving your action or efforts.

Next, as a group, consider what behaviors or practices are needed to achieve those values. There may be some new systems that will be needed and other, older practices that will need to be revised. You and your team may even want to scrap some practices that are obstacles to achievement of the values.

Ask your employees, "What are the obstacles to implementation of these values within our department?" Your staff may not be able to come up with ways to eliminate those obstacles, but once you know what they are, you can find ways to change the norms that conflict with the values.

Later, in one-on-one sessions with your staff members, you'll want to define the roles of each in achieving the value set. At that time, you both may also want to review the employee's job description to determine if there are any conflicts between the employee's existing responsibilities and the values. What should be done? Maybe the responsibilities need to be rethought. Remember the situation with the plant buyer. Installation of a computer system that enabled the plant to practice J-I-T *and* never experience downtime might have resolved his dilemma. Too expensive? Maybe a meeting between the buyer, his manager, and the production supervisor with the loud voice would have clarified the plant's goals. With assurances from the buyer that every effort would be made to track supplies, the production manager might have learned to be more understanding about shortages—particularly if he saw the dollar savings from more careful management of inventory.

Incorporate the values into your employees' performance appraisal interviews, as well. Set outcomes or key results or ratings that reflect the values, and monitor employee performance in these areas.

Your Role in Value-Based Departments

Keep in mind how important it is that your own behaviors be in sync with those values that your corporation or department has set to guide it. Here are some suggestions:

• *Role model the values your company has set.* Just as you wouldn't get your employees to pursue department goals if they didn't see you doing your fair share, so you can't expect your employees to support the values being promulgated if they don't see you doing so.

Depending on your values, ask yourself:

1. Do I treat my internal customers with the same respect as I treat external customers?
2. Do I show by my words and actions that risk taking and creative thinking are appreciated?
3. What about risks that fail? Do I truly behave as if I believe that mistakes are learning experiences?
4. How do I reinforce these values, in words and in actions?
5. How do I support our company's concern about total quality?
6. How do I demonstrate my support of empowerment?
7. Do I truly understand and practice teamwork?

If you aren't walking the walk, then it isn't likely that your employees will support the values. That includes putting your budget where your mouth is—devoting dollars to see that the values are achieved and other dollars, if you can, to recognize those who support the values.

• *Get feedback from others about your management style.* If your company has people values, you may need someone other than yourself to make a judgment about how well you practice them.

"Self-centered," "untrustworthy," and "manipulative" are all words that employees commonly use to refer to bosses who practice fear management, that is, managers who humiliate and malign workers with the idea that they will perform at a higher level rather than risk having their names at the top of the list for the next wave of layoffs. Fear management takes many forms: threats, personal attacks, public humiliation, and indifference to employees' personal problems.

We think we're practicing tough-love supervision, but in actuality we're demoralizing workers to the point that they can't perform.

Feedback from a trusted assistant or peer can also alert you to failure to meet values associated with customer service, collaboration, change management, innovation and risk taking, and worknetting (see Chapter 10). Marge may not know that she is a red-taper when it comes to customer problems, or Herb, who heads systems, may be unaware of how curt he can be to systems users when they call with problems; Dan won't say yes to anything new unless it is thoroughly vetted by everyone within the organization; Calvin comes close to being antisocial with the very people his department needs to get its projects done. Look for someone you can trust in your organization to give you a 360-degree assessment about how you fare with the values; then develop a personal action plan to change your ways where necessary so that your norms are in sync with the values you are promoting.

- *Encourage the role modeling of the values throughout your entire company.* If you're the only one who puts the values into behaviors, your employees are more likely to see you as a chump than as a hero. Better that every manager practice the behaviors associated with the values.

Sam is a supervisor in a midwestern plant. Recently, the plant set some values, one of which was to identify opportunities for partnerships with other crews and pursue these to the benefit of the organization. Sam seems to be the only supervisor who has heard the message. At least, no one so far has agreed to bring his team to a joint meeting with Sam's to improve workflow. Rather than be annoyed with the other supervisors, Sam's own crew seems more embarrassed about Sam. "Give it up, Sam," Dick, his crew chief, told him. "We don't need their help; they clearly think they don't need ours. Anything we want to get done we can do on our own."

Sam knows otherwise. To get his colleagues to meet with him, he sent them all an e-mail message that outlined a way all could benefit if they worked together. Of the four, only one didn't show up. Sam had his plan outlined, but he pointed out that it was something that required all the teams' participation. And at that meeting, all four of Sam's colleagues' teams were present to discuss the project, fine-tune the idea, and develop an action plan. Sam's colleagues saw how everyone could come out winners by participating in this project—and, incidentally, they did. Which made it easier for Sam to bring team members together the next time.

• *Provide a payoff.* Once behaviors are tied to goals, it is possible to tie raises and rewards to achievement of goals. This is also true for values. Generally behavior doesn't change if employees don't see a benefit—a payoff.

• *Communicate, communicate, communicate.* Critical to the old MBO programs was continuous communication of the goals. Values are goals, and they also need to be regularly talked about if you are to see them achieved.

When an employee does something in keeping with a value, acknowledge her. But also use that occasion to review all the values, not just the one the employee followed.

Values aren't a fad. They are the principles that determine how you want your company to work, the parameters within which your empowered employees can operate, the goals that are critical to your company's survival. And you can overcome problems you might be having getting employee buy-in by practicing the same good management you practice in traditional goal setting.

9

Scaling Invisible Walls: Learning How to Span Functions

In the early 1990s, as companies reorganized, many around teams, the expectation was that the functional silos that made communication between departments difficult would disappear. Bringing down the walls and flattening the organizations would encourage greater communication and collaboration between different areas.

But restructuring around teams hasn't entirely eliminated the silos; rather, we have new silos—the cross-functional teams that are a part of our more collaborative culture. True, now that Departments A and C have representatives on the same cross-functional team (CFT), they do cooperate and communicate more. But, on the other hand, Department B has no members on that team, so neither A nor C communicates with B; in the past they didn't, and they still don't, although a more cooperative relationship among all three could mean more efficient operation for each department and ultimately greater competitive advantage for the company.

The Problem

The problem is that the communication paths that existed before the reorganization and restructuring haven't changed as dramatically as was hoped. Either managers don't recognize the advantages from expanding their collegial networks or creating department or team alliances or partnerships, or they lack the skills to create these relationships.

Breakfast, Anyone?

Clark heads up marketing for his company's line of hot cereals. Will is product manager of the same company's cold breakfast treats. Both lead teams within their organization. Recently a competitor came out with a breakfast muffin that could be served hot or cold. Clark's team and Will's group had both thought of something like this, but neither group pursued it because each thought its development belonged to the other.

When Clark heard about the competitor's product introduction from one of his sales reps, he called Will. "Why didn't your group move with this idea?" he angrily asked. "It should have been evident that people wanted a breakfast meal they could serve either hot or cold that wasn't a cereal. We have known there was a market for it for some time, but. . . ."

"So why didn't you recommend that the company develop and test market such a product?" Will asked.

"Because it wasn't the kind of product our group usually markets," Clark answered.

"Well, it wasn't ours, either."

After both calmed down and drew together in their common enmity to their company's competitor, both managers agreed to get their groups together immediately to develop a suitable competitive product.

"I still don't know how we failed to come up with this product," Will said before he hung up the phone.

The answer to Will's question is simple: Members of Will's and Clark's groups speak to each other, but neither group's members spoke to the other team's members about the idea. Communications has increased among team members but not across teams. Clark's and Will's teams are as much silos in that respect as the functional silos they were created to eliminate.

If you drew lines on the organization chart to reflect the

communication that Clark and Will have with each other and with colleagues over time, you find that they infrequently speak to each other and to a lot of other people who could make the jobs of these two managers easier. It's not that either Clark or Will is antisocial; both managers have friends within the organization. It's just that neither has seen the advantage of regular informal contact with the other or, for that matter, with others outside their existing social circle to help them with their jobs. Nor have either of these managers encouraged their staff members to network with other staff members within the organization.

Creating new communication channels with peers has to be a deliberate effort, something you put on your to-do list along with completing a major proposal or holding a counseling session with a problem employee. Similar priority has to be given to developing partnerships between your team and others.

Neither Will nor Clark has suggested to the other a joint meeting of their teams; neither has invited members of another team to one of his team's sessions to learn about a success of the visiting team or to discuss a need of the visiting team that his group could help meet. Until this situation arose, neither manager had seen how an alliance between his team and another could help their company. This isn't the only occasion where Clark's and Will's isolationism has meant a lost opportunity for revenue growth. The two teams have also lost out on other opportunities. Last month, for instance, Will's group decided that it really could benefit from a customer study about one of its products, but the team decided to defer the study until it could afford to hire researchers to go to the stores that sold the product to interview potential customers.

Clark runs a department made up of forty sales reps who sell to around 400 regional stores, all of which carry that product. These sales reps could have completed a survey of Will's group of store managers or overseen a more sophisticated customer study, if Clark had known about Will's need.

WIIFM

In forming alliances or partnerships (or "worknets," to differentiate these contacts from external networking for purposes of

career advancement), you can demonstrate your own commitment to corporate teamwork. This can increase your opportunities for advancement in two ways. First, companies are looking
for team players, managers who demonstrate a willingness to
collaborate with others for both their department's and others'
advantage. Second, and more directly, the cooperation of others
will enable you to achieve your department's objectives or goals,
which certainly makes you a better candidate for advancement
than those who don't make the bottom line.

Imagine the opportunities from building collaborative relationships with other managers. You could negotiate with a colleague to provide you with an additional hand to complete a
project, someone within her department who has just the skills
you need. Or someone in your organization may have a need for
the same office technology that you want but that you can't
make a strong enough case for purchasing solely for your department. Given your mutual need, you will be able to more
than justify the expense. Or you may have an idea that would
provide a new distribution channel. If you have the support of
peers in planning as well as of some members of senior management who can help push your idea through, your proposal will
receive approval—and your department will have a new revenue stream.

The Worth of Worknets, Alliances, and Partnerships

Worknets, alliances, and partnerships mean:

- *Information.* It can be information that provides an answer
to a specific problem or help in making a decision right now,
such as which of two new data systems to contract for. When
the worknet extends outside your company's boundaries, to
suppliers or customers, it can alert you to trends or developments. The larger your worknet, the better your opportunity to
discover what you need to know while you can still do something about the situation.

- *Feedback.* Before you submit that proposal for a new product or service, you can test it on those distributors or customers who are a part of your external worknet. If you have an idea for improving operating efficiency, you can test it on peers. In either situation, your idea might have been rejected, but early feedback could have prevented you from submitting a bad proposal or provided you with insights to help fine-tune an idea that, when rethought, might fly.

• *A psychological boost.* That feeling of optimism can come even if it stems simply from recognition that you aren't the only one with a problem or concern; you're not alone in your concern or fear. This sense of belonging—even when it only means that the same things that give you nightmares are giving colleagues nighmares or that you and your colleagues share a mutual dislike (remember how Clark and Will came together when they talked about the company's competition)—can allow you to put your fear or anger aside and cope with a situation.

• *A mine of resources.* You can use your alliance to get the money, equipment, and other assistance your team needs to accomplish its goals. And your team, knowing that resources will be available to it, is likely to be more motivated, willing to accept goals that involve greater stretch.

Back to the Basics

In the past, networks, alliances, and partnerships referred to arrangements with individuals and organizations outside your company, not teams and colleagues within it. Negotiations were over provisions in union agreements, not how you and a colleague could both win by working in concert. But lessons learned from these earlier situations can be applied today to build collaborative relationships with others within your organization that will enable you and your team to accomplish great things for your company—things you couldn't do at all if you tried to do them on your own.

Relationship Building

Networking was the means by which you advanced your career. You looked for people who were influential in your field. You searched them out at association meetings, trade shows, or civic meetings, and you schmoozed with them because these people knew other people or could themselves recommend you for a better job elsewhere. Maybe they were individuals in your industry, or maybe they were people in your field. You wanted as many solid contacts as you could get, should you need help in locating another job.

If you found yourself in a career bind, you could also call these individuals to get an objective view of the situation. Not only might these people know someone who had a job for you, they could build your self-esteem when you were feeling low by telling you how great you are.

Similarly, companies formed alliances and partnerships with other divisions or companies to enter a new marketplace, produce a new product, or otherwise increase both companies' competitive positions. These arrangements were successful only if both parties could gain something from the deal. Those who were successful at this were those who negotiated not only to gain what they wanted but to ensure that the other organization also achieved its objective. They knew not to make negotiations into a power game in which they might win the battle but lose a relationship with another company that could better position their organization.

Alliances, partnerships, and, yes, even networks involved study of the potential contact's needs and interests and consideration of how you could help with them, for it was recognized that such relationships were built on reciprocity. Just as senior management might study a company's annual report and business projections before contracting for a formal relationship, managers skilled at networking considered carefully those individuals who might best help their professional growth in selecting those to be a part of their networks. They developed their networks the same way they ran their departments—in a very concise, organized fashion.

They checked out those who might be at a business function who could help with their career, then identified what those people had in common with them. Mutual interests enabled them to start a conversation with these people that wasn't work-related. While schmoozing, they would suggest exchanging business cards, just in case. A few days later, they would follow up that casual conversation with a call or a letter, maybe with a suggestion for lunch.

At lunch, they would identify how they could help out the other person and how willing, in return, that person would be to maintain the contact in the interest of mutual assistance.

You included the names of members in your network in your Rolodex and made a point to phone each at least once every few months to set up a lunch date or just to socialize for a few minutes. You listened to their complaints and, if you saw a way you could help the person, you offered it, because it reinforced the relationship. If you thought the person could help you, you asked, knowing that a network is a give-and-take relationship; if you didn't ask for help, the other person would infer that you didn't think he had anything to offer.

Interpersonal Skills

To sustain these outside relationships, you used the same inter-personal skills you used to build rapport with your boss or em-ployees. Interpersonal skills were important to relationships with those inside your organization above and below you, not sideways; in the past, peers were competitors for the job you wanted.

In your communications with your boss, employees, and colleagues outside your organization (partners, allies, or net-work contacts), you were:

- *Watchful of the other person's needs and concerns.* If you could help, you would. At the very least, you would listen to their problems.

- *Sincere.* You wanted the other person to know you could be trusted to keep your word if you made a promise. So you worked hard to build a reputation for following through on any commitments you made to others.

- *Confident.* You did your homework whenever you could so that you could be self-confident. The more impressed individ-uals are with your credentials, the easier it is to influence them to do things your way. Similarly, the more outsiders know about your expertise, the more they want to be a part of your career network.

• *Flexible.* Executives had to be willing to change their negotiating plan if they wanted the other company's negotiators to change theirs. Likewise, in dealing with their bosses, managers soon learned that being hard-nosed about an issue would get them nowhere. Better to say to your boss, "I'm not sure I agree. Could you share with me your thinking?" With employees, you listened to their ideas and gave them serious consideration before making the decision about how to approach a situation.

• *Congenial.* No one wants to schmooze with a gloomy Gus or someone who is always adversarial or even someone who comes across as politically savvy. Better to keep the atmosphere in interactions friendly and nonadversarial. The point networkers wanted to make, and managers wanted to make with their employees, and, to some extent, supervisors and managers wanted to make to their bosses, too, was: "If we can work this out, you'll get what you want in return. We'll both be contented. How about it?"

This certainly is the attitude of the best union and management negotiators. They go into discussions with the objective of finding common ground and then building on it to address other problems. They know what issues they won't negotiate on and which less important issues they can be flexible about. They certainly try to understand how the other party thinks by listening closely to what she says, as well as by attending to her nonverbal communications. They don't argue over minor issues, and they deal with issues as they arise so they don't get in the way of a final agreement. Most of all, they are persistent, raising questions to keep discussion going in order to find that common ground in which both parties can begin the process of collaboration.

Fad Solutions

In today's organizations, with resources scarce, worknets, alliances, and partnerships among managers may be critical to getting work done. Unfortunately, many managers don't realize the value of developing collaborative relationships with their colleagues.

Where worknets exist, they just seem to happen. Managers haven't learned to look at their organizations and first determine who within their companies can help them or their teams accomplish their missions, then contact and begin to create a relationship that might develop into an effective alliance or partnership.

Perhaps as a holdover from the past, there seems to be a reluctance on the part of some managers to ask colleagues for help. They worry that senior executives will think that they can't handle their own problems. They aren't wise enough to know that no one expects them to have all the answers or that they could gain corporate points in today's collaborative workplace by being a team player.

There is another problem. While advocating more collaborative relationships among their managers, companies haven't devoted time or money to train them in the interpersonal skills they need to create worknets, ally themselves with other colleagues, or partner their team with other teams. Senior managements of these companies think that such collaboration is a natural by-product of the restructuring. But teams, just like the departments before them, can easily develop an "us versus them" mentality unless their leaders model cooperative behavior.

Failure to provide the training can be costly. A partnership created by managers or teams—a process that can take considerable time—can easily break down during implementation for any of a number of reasons, from personality conflicts to differences in opinion about either the means or ends to achieve the final result. These rips in the relationships could be repaired, but they often aren't, and the projects die because managers were unable to rebuild the relationships because of their poor interpersonal skills.

The ongoing downsizings have also created situations that demand greater collaboration between operating areas within the organization.

Jay is a senior vice president at a telecommunications firm.

Although he is headquartered in Rochester, New York, he also has responsibility for operation of the firm's Des Moines facility. He supervises four managers there because of a corporate downsizing that meant the layoff of several middle and senior managers.

At first the four managers in Des Moines were delighted to report to someone from headquarters and be merged into the Rochester department. But soon they discovered that Jay, given his new responsibilities for the merged operation and his special tasks for the CEO, had very little time for them. If they were to succeed, they had to depend on their own resources.

Jay would like to take time to speak to each of his reports in Des Moines, but he can spend only about two days every two weeks in the midwest center, as much of his time is spent putting out fires or attending management meetings as the representative of the firm's CEO. So Jay is delighted that his four managers meet once a month for lunch to share problems and successes with each other. If one or the other has had a few minutes with Jay, that person can share what was said with the others. But more often they talk about needs they have that another of the managers can help with. Jay knows he isn't giving the managers the time they need, but his hectic work schedule has led to a partnership in the Des Moines facility that may be doing much more for the managers than a few hours with him each month could do. The four don't dislike Jay—they are just frustrated by their inability to get his time. But due to this mutual irritation with his schedule, Dan, Sara, Becky, and Donna have formed their own alliance, supporting one another with advice, shared resources, and whatever one department or another needs, in defense against further downsizing.

Jay's situation also reflects another postdownsizing situation—the merging of two independent operations into a single entity.

The Rochester and Des Moines operations have been combined into a single division on the organization chart, but both groups continue to think of themselves as separate divisions. The Des Moines operation is very tight-knit whereas the Rochester group is made up of managers who operate more independently of one another. There are opportunities for revenue through cooperation between the two groups, but Jay needs to build a camaraderie between the two divergent operations if his company is to see those profits. Jay's groups are geographically distant, which adds to his problem, but even merged groups that operate down the hall from each other have found it difficult to identify and work together on projects that offer mutual benefits. The relationship between the two groups resembles a Smothers Brothers routine, with Des Moines' managers (Tom) continually complaining that Jay ("Mom") likes Rochester (Dick) more.

The Balancing Act

If you are to get your job and that of your team done, you may need to have good relations not only with your boss and employees but your colleagues. The secret to getting cooperation from your associates is much the same as the secret to winning cooperation from your employees: find out what they want most from their work, then satisfy these desires. It is also the secret of good labor negotiations and good merger or partner negotiations.

But first you have to get to know those within your organization who can best help you. To do this, follow these guidelines:

• *Allocate the time to create a worknet.* You have to make a conscious effort to form alliances, just as in the past managers made a conscious effort to know those outside their organizations who could help their careers or pinpoint potential corporate partners.

Keep in mind how easy it is to forget the need for those casual conversations that can reveal key information to help your team, or how easily you can forget to set up a lunch date with a colleague that might enable you at some point to ask her support for an idea you want to implement. So set aside time in your calendar for the informal communications that pave the way for worknets and alliances.

• *Assess your current contacts.* In the past, networkers maintained a list of contacts and made some effort to identify in advance those they wanted to add to their net before casting it out. Today's managers' allies likely come by chance—being in the right place at the right time to either help you or be helped by you. If your current worknet won't satisfy all your job needs or team's job needs (and in today's organizations it's unlikely it will), then you will need to begin consciously growing your worknet.

• *Focus on the most important alliances and relationships.* You can't be friends with everyone—there isn't enough time for you to incorporate everyone into your worknet and, besides, it wouldn't be advantageous to do so. The networkers of the 1960s, 1970s, and 1980s realized that you made a commitment to members of your net, and you couldn't expand your network indefinitely and still satisfy those commitments.

In building alliances, partnerships, and worknets, you want to build relationships with those people who are most critical to what you want to accomplish. Again, emulate what those who created career-focused networks did by taking an organized approach. Begin with a list of people you deal with daily. Don't exclude those you don't like or have poor relationships with. Just the opposite; put stars next to these people's names. Then review the list, dividing the individuals into three categories: those people without whom you couldn't do your work; those people who make it easier for you to do your work; and those incidental relationships that don't directly affect your work. You should spend most of your time sustaining and/or building relationships with those who can help you or your team the most, almost as much time with those who are important to your team and you, and any leftover time with those who are incidental to your work and that of your team.

One manager began to build a worknet by first looking at his own strengths and weaknesses. Then he identified those peers within the organization who were strong in areas where this manager was weak. These were the first individuals he made a point of chatting with at the next office social event.

• *Look for ways to make allies out of enemies.* If you both share a common problem, just acknowledging it may be sufficient to help bring down the walls and begin the process of building a bridge between you. Common enemies or troubles can make friends. Besides, once you get to know this person and she gets to know you, you may find you like each other and enjoy working together.

• *Become an expert in the art of schmoozing.* Schmoozing is engaging in light conversation for the purpose of making a permanent and positive impression. At company social events or business meetings, identify those individuals you don't know and make it a point to get to meet them. Don't limit the conversation to business issues. Find out about their interests. If you have common ones, so much the better. But keep these interests in mind so that the next time you see the individual, you can raise the topic again. If you want to add this person to your worknet, you can ask about it when you call before inviting the person to lunch.

• *Keep in touch.* Once you've made contact, maintain that contact. Even small talk can be better than no talk at all. You'll be emulating the networkers of the past who sustained their career networks by not letting their initial contacts fall by the wayside, or the senior executives who kept in touch with those with whom they contracted corporate partnerships or alliances to identify further opportunities.

• *Don't depend solely on the new technology to communicate.* As I mention in Chapter 6, we often use the new technology to avoid one-on-one communication. When it comes to building relationships, there are numerous ways we can communicate other than in person—reports, letters, memos, and e-mail. But these aren't as effective as in-person contact in building interpersonal relationships or addressing problems with worknet members.

• *Cultivate a power base.* Power comes from a willingness to share credit, a desire to lend a hand as well as get a hand, and a willingness to give access to information as well as gain access to information. This kind of power stems from feelings of trust that you earn when you share the glory with those who helped you achieve your goal, demonstrate that you can be trusted not only to lend the hand you promised but to keep confidential those things told you by a worknet member, and give credit to members within your network without expecting them to recognize your contribution.

- *Be prepared to share and share alike with members of your worknet.* Remember that resources you need for a task may be held by another person; sharing the resources at your disposal with this person may encourage him to share resources he has with you.

- *Keep the issue of reciprocity in your mind.* It's relevant in building individual worknets or team partnerships or alliances, just as it has always been critical in negotiating corporate alliances or partnerships or adding to your career net.

You need to ask yourself, "What will the other party's payback be from helping me and my team?" and "What will my payback be from helping my colleague?"

One manager had a colleague who would help out because, she said, "she was a good corporate citizen," but she also used her past favors to get help when she needed it.

The payback can take different forms, depending on the individual. It might be access to critical resources, staff assistance, assumption of an unwanted task, cooperation that enables quicker completion of a project, equal recognition for the project completed, an opportunity to meet or work with other partners, personal or emotional backing when the need exists, or even ownership of a newly developing work area. You have to consider both what you are willing to give and what you would want in return from a member of your worknet.

Negotiating for help should be win/win—that is, mutually beneficial. You should consider yourself and your colleague or your team and his team partners in solving a problem. Don't be reluctant to ask a peer for help. You don't want to constantly have your hand out—over time, even the most avid team player can grow weary of lending help—but asking for assistance from a colleague in her area of expertise is evidence of the respect you have for her ability. But be prepared to follow the suggestion; going to someone for advice but not following it is a waste of both your time and hers.

When you approach a colleague to work with you on a project or to support your idea in some way:

- *State your needs clearly.* Identify not only what you need from your peer but the benefits to your peer of helping you. In any negotiations, as seasoned labor negotiators know, it is important to recognize that the needs and concerns of both parties are legitimate and of equal importance and that any final solution must reflect both persons' interests.

- *Be prepared to hear your colleague out.* Old-time negotiators will tell you that they didn't win in the first few minutes of discussion. They had to be prepared for refusal at first. So be prepared to listen to your colleague without interruption. And don't be thinking of how to rebut the points your colleague is making as he is speaking. Your goal is to find some common ground from which you can build a partnership.

- *Identify areas of mutual need.* Focus first on getting agreement on the situation and fully understanding your colleague's needs and interests before searching for a solution both of you can live with. Shared needs and interests can be the foundation for development of a solution to your problem.

- *Explain the "why."* Having a fuller understanding of the reason for your need may make it easier for your colleague to evaluate the pros and cons of various work relationships that might give you or your team the hand it needs.

- *Be as flexible as possible.* Maybe your peer can't lend you his computer expert for a week. Find out why not. Maybe you can reach a compromise. Maybe you can get the use of the staff member for two days in return for providing his department with clerical support on a problem it is having.

- *If you can't agree on the big issues, try to find agreement on the small ones.* This can give you a collaborative foundation from which you can address the more important concerns at a later time.

- *Look for verbal and nonverbal clues to discover how your colleague is reacting to your idea.* Maybe the individual's first response was to talk about how helping you would make it impossible for her to achieve important outcomes for her department at the end of the year. Ask yourself what you can do to help her make those year-end goals.

Watch body language, too, to see if it is in sync with the verbal message. Arms crossed or legs crossed may be a sign of defensiveness, even of an unwillingness to listen, whereas leaning toward you suggests an interest or enthusiasm. Nonverbal cues are as important to monitor in interpersonal communications as the content of the conversations to identify how to negotiate with the person to achieve your ends.

These are important interpersonal skills you need to master:

• *Ask questions.* It is how you make worknet contacts to begin with. It is how you sustain them. And it is also how you move beyond that level to partner with peers on projects and other change initiatives.

Ask what you can do to help the other person when she points to a problem in her department that prevents her team from helping yours. One bit of advice: Avoid asking the other party specifically why she won't do something to help you. Asking the "why" question can put the individual on the defensive. If you can, redirect the discussion away from why the other person can't help you to how you both can collaborate and what you can do for each other.

Listen to the answers to your questions, and where necessary ask other questions for clearer communication. Let's say, for instance, a colleague and you are discussing how to create a new database. She has suggested an end run around the head of systems, something you strongly disagree with. Rather than reject that suggestion outright, you might ask first, "Why do you think that would work better than going to Stan, the department's head?" Maybe another team leader has proposed a meeting of both groups. "I'll issue the invitations," he tells you. You like the idea of a joint meeting but would like to jointly invite the groups to the meeting. You might ask, "How will you phrase the invitation?" then follow up his answer with your own suggestions, followed by another question, "How do you think these points would fit with your ideas?"

• *Use silence effectively.* We all like audiences, whether it is to share our accomplishments or to hear our side of some problem situation. Be willing to be the other person's audience. Sometimes the worst thing you can do is to interrupt someone who is venting about a situation to share a similar situation you encountered or interrupt someone who is taking bows about an accomplishment to showcase your own accomplishment.

Wait until the individual is through; then make your request again, keeping in mind what you have just heard from the individual. There should be a way to help the other person. Even if it doesn't lead to his helping you with this project, it may lead to his assisting you on some other project at a later time.

• *Become aware of the rules by which your colleagues operate.* Listen for words like *must* or *can't* or *shouldn't*. It doesn't matter if the judgments are valid (that is, based on corporate policy) or if they simply reflect the other party's mindset; they are the constraints you have to keep in mind in any alliances or partnerships with this person and her team.

• *Monitor resistance.* When you're trying to use your influence, you may get some foot-dragging. The person isn't saying no to you; it's more like, "We'll see." To make this person an ally or partner with you on a project, you may have to make further concessions or provide more information or reassurances that the effort you two are considering will succeed.

• *Overcome insecurities by getting them on the table.* Identify them; then refocus attention away from them. Maybe your colleague is afraid of joining with you on a project because of the risks of failure. Point to the benefits, not only to the organization but to your career and to your ally's position within the organization. The benefits have to outweigh the risks in the minds of potential partners or allies for them to agree to collaborate on a project.

• *Seek entrainment.* Entrainment is matching or mirroring the other party's voice, gestures, or movements. Subtly emulating your colleague's style of communication can help to establish a rapport that helps you influence the other person's response. If someone else is using entrainment on you, on the other hand, and you find yourself being drawn into a deal that you would rather avoid, you can easily break the entrainment by destroying the synchronicity—either look at your watch or break eye contact, or maybe stand up if the other party is seated.

• *Address problems in relationships as soon as they occur.* You don't have to confront the person if he lets you down. Rather, you can approach him for "input" to get a better perspective on what happened. That's what Sylvia did after a derogatory remark that her coworker, Marge, made about Sylvia's staff in front of Sylvia's boss.

Sylvia thought Marge would support her recommendation that the marketing department participate in the November trade show in Los Angeles. But Marge was one of the team reporting to Marshall Stern who vetoed the idea. More startling, however, was Marge's comment to Sylvia following the meeting. Marshall was with them, and Marge told Sylvia in front of Marshall how poorly she felt Sylvia's group had covered a booth during the trade show in New Orleans.

Sylvia was speechless. She appreciated the feedback, since she hadn't been to the show, but, given their comfortable working relationship, Sylvia felt that Marge should have mentioned it to her privately before bringing it to Marshall's attention. Everyone knew how uptight he could get about criticism of any of his staff. All weekend the comment nagged her.

On Monday, Sylvia called Marge and suggested that they have lunch together. Marge agreed. Sylvia put aside the small talk to get to the heart of the problem immediately.

"Why," she asked, "did you use that occasion to let me know how poorly the team had covered the show? If there was a problem, I should have been told sooner. I'm asking not because I'm angry but because I want input to help our ongoing relationship. What have I done or said to make you think that we could not have worked this problem out together? I haven't been comfortable with our relationship since Friday when you told Marshall how poorly my group behaved at the last trade show. I'd like to know what they did and what behaviors from me prompted you to bring the problem up in front of my boss."

"Well," Marge replied, "the last time I mentioned a problem with show coverage, you told me you would take care of it. But you didn't, and I don't want a repetition at the next show."

Sylvia considered Marge a friend but, more important, she regarded Marge as a critical member of her worknet. She felt that an apology was in order—from her, for her failure to respond to Marge's initial complaint, and from Marge, for using the occasion to make Sylvia look bad.

"You're right. I should have done something about the problem. But I think you could have brought the issue to my attention in private."

"I guess it was unfair to bring it up in front of your boss," she said, "particularly since I knew you weren't there and likely had no idea what had happened. Next time, I'll talk to you first. But if you knew what happened, you would understand how angry I was."

"Well, what did happen?" Sylvia asked.

Marge then went on to share with Sylvia the problems that had occurred and that she expected Sylvia to avoid in the future.

The conversation is interesting because it shows how you can use your interpersonal skills to address a collegial problem without alienating your associate.

First, Sylvia found a time when she and Marge could talk, and she immediately got to the point, thereby communicating to Marge how important what had happened was to her, with her remark, "I haven't been comfortable with our relationship since Friday when you told me in front of my boss how poorly my group had performed at the last trade show. I'd like to know what they did wrong and what behaviors from me prompted you to bring the problem up with my boss before talking to me about them."

Sylvia was angry, but she didn't let it prevent her restoring her relationship with Marge. Rather, Sylvia focused on learning more about Marge's concerns and improving their relationship. Her communication style was also very effective.

Sylvia referred to "we" and "I," not "you," throughout her conversation with Marge. She also paused after stating her concern to see how Marge was responding to her words. She prefaced her own observations with the phrases "I feel" and "It seemed to me" to show Marge that she was reflecting her own feelings and no one else's. She was wise not to draw the discussion into a confrontation in which she began to fingerpoint with words like "You always do this" or "You can never be counted on to support others."

If you don't feel that you can be as cool and calm as Sylvia in a similar situation, ask a third person to be present, to act as mediator as you resolve your differences and reinstate the previous work relationship. Handling bumps in your relationships with worknet members can be difficult. Sometimes it is a trial-and-error process in which you learn how best to work with a colleague by doing something wrong—like Sylvia, who did not respond immediately to Marge's initial complaint.

Team Relationships

In team-based organizations or organizations with CFTs, you will want to develop partnerships with other teams. Toward this, you'll need to:

- *Hold informal meetings between your teams and other teams within the organization that provide work to you or for whom you do work.* These sessions make a great opportunity to exchange information with colleagues or to identify solutions to problems you or the other group are encountering. It's a process that heads of companies undertake before making overtures toward a partnership or alliance.

- *Strengthen your department's ability to network.* Give assignments to your staff that enable them to grow their networking skills. Let's say you have a project that has to be done with another department. Why not ask one of your staff members to arrange for the meeting and handle other details with the group?

- *Build a team of team leaders that will help you all.* That's what Jay's direct reports did when they found they couldn't always depend on Jay to be available to help them.

Team leaders who meet regularly and are supportive of each other can exchange resources faster and more efficiently than they could if contacts were more informal.

- *Don't limit your team contacts to those within the organization.* Develop partnerships with your critical teams at supplier and customer companies. This will give your staff members individuals with whom they can work when problems arise. They can turn to members of these external networks for answers to their questions, for information, and for help in expediting shipments and paperwork to make everyone's job easier.

Merged Groups

What if you find yourself, like Jay, with two operations that now must work as one? You should:

• *Develop a mission and plan for the new group with representatives from both operations.* If your company practices bottom-up planning, the annual planning session is an excellent opportunity to get the group thinking as a single team. Consider the written mission statement like a partnership between two separate organizations that have agreed to work together. Over time, the need for it will disappear. But initially it gives direction to the new work relationship.

• *Begin immediately.* If the merger was traumatic and included the loss of some key staff members, you may want to give the group a few weeks to adjust to the new work relationship. During these few weeks, you should take the opportunity to communicate as frequently as possible with your new reports—another trick out of the book of those skilled in successful acquisitions and mergers.

These conversations will also enable you to gauge when the employees are emotionally able to discuss the future and you can share with the merged group your vision for the future.

• *Stress the importance of both informal and formal contacts between members of the previously separate groups.* If the groups have worked informally together, recognize that, and encourage further collaborative efforts. But also plan to hold regular formal meetings with the new group in which you share progress on the accomplishments of each and on some collaborative efforts.

• *Find opportunities to work together.* This may be the toughest task, but it is also the most critical. You need to get the two groups working on a project together. This likely means that you will have to help them identify an opportunity in which both will see payback. One successful joint endeavor should make the team members willing to do it again.

You may have to help them initially find these opportunities, perhaps by holding some joint brainstorming sessions. But in time they should see the wisdom of working more closely together.

10

The First Step to Virtual Organizations: Practicing Distance Management

The Information Age is changing the work environment of the late twentieth century as dramatically as the Industrial Revolution changed the work environment of the late nineteenth century. But this time the new technology is the personal computer, which is making it possible for employees to move out of their offices to work at home or in work centers nearer their home either full- or part-time, even as the equipment of the Industrial Revolution moved employees from their homes, where they did piecework, to factories.

Estimates differ as to how many employees today telecommute, but projections suggest that the number could exceed 9 million by the end of this century.

This movement to the virtual organization, where few people, if any, will work regularly in an office but instead will be linked by phone and computer to one another and, maybe, to one or more work centers, represents a major change for your organization and you.

You probably moved up in a workplace where you were located only a few feet from your boss. Now, as a boss yourself, you may find yourself overseeing the work of people both a few feet away and many miles away. For both kinds of employees, the need for supervision is the same, but for the latter group there is the issue of how you will manage individuals you infrequently see.

Building Staff On-Line

Marty, an entrepreneur, has built his organization with the help of ten employees whom he has seen maybe twice in the four years he has been growing his business. More one-on-one meetings—maybe once a week or every two weeks—would have been better, but Marty has learned to work effectively with this staff he never sees. His business shows companies how to apply the new office technology, which means that Marty is comfortable with sending e-mail from one site to another and other on-line capabilities. Still, even Marty admitted to me that it took some adjusting to this different work arrangement and a change in the way he manages.

The Problem

Since you can't observe your employees at work, you can't determine how long it takes them to do their work, and consequently you can't measure their productivity. When your employees are within your sight, you can at least be certain that they are at their desks or at meetings. But telework takes that assurance away, which may be why many managers still resist the idea. Indeed, at a time when so many employees telework, managers of conventional workers still worry about letting a single employee work at home one day to deal with a delivery or cope with some plumbing problem, rather than take the day off as a vacation day.

Teleworking Issues to Address

The possible abuse of the privilege of working at home by cheating a company of hours is one of several management issues that managers will need to contend with. Incidentally, an employee may not deliberately fail to put in the required hours but rather may have too many distractions at home—from family chores, to the TV, to neighbors who drop by to chat—to focus on his job. But how do you raise the issue of trust? It may make you uncomfortable about asking for proof that the work is getting done, but what other options do you have?

Another problem in supervising teleworkers is balancing workload, schedules of employees who work on-site and at home, and their accessibility to others while on-site to ensure coordination of work and communication of work progress.

Telecommuters themselves complain about the isolation that comes from working at home—the feeling of being cut off from the rest of the team at the office—and the lack of input and feedback that are also a part of the traditional workplace.

Still another possible problem is the loss of employee loyalty, which may go so far as to encourage teleworkers to "sunlight," that is, work for others during their telecommuting days.

Some of these problems happened to Bill when he OK'd telecommuting for three of his ten employees.

Bill had looked carefully at the economics when he was approached by the staff members about letting them work at home. The economics—decreased overhead costs from the savings in workspace—made sense. So did the management issues; organizations that have tried telecomuting have reported noticeable increases in productivity and work satisfaction. So Bill agreed to let Margie, Larry, and Tim all work at home. Each had a personal reason for the request, and Bill's agreement was well received.

For Margie, it meant that she could stay home with her ailing mother yet still work full-time; her mother would not have to go to a nursing home. For Larry, it meant that his wife could take a job, thereby bringing in a second paycheck and enabling them to send their disabled son to a special school. And for Tim, divorced and with custody of his five-year-old daughter, it meant that he could deliver her to her school, pick her up at the end of the school day, and have a few hours of playtime with her before bedtime.

Bill was able to get financing from senior management to

equip each of the employees with the technology that he or she would need to do the work at home. The company saw this as an important experiment and was willing to pay for the desktop computers, systems software, designated fax lines, sophisticated telephone lines with voice mail retrieval, e-mail, and access to the Internet. Bill had been very persuasive.

For the first few weeks, everything went well. The three employees had each agreed to come to the office for at least two hours each week, and Bill was initially pleased with the reports he heard. But by the fourth week, he began to hear, too, about problems. These reports came, not from the three telecommuters, but from customers and colleagues with whom they worked.

Margie, a customer service rep who handled five major accounts for the company, didn't seem to be available to callers, Bill was told by a buyer. Calls to three other purchasing agents whose business she handled revealed the same problem. Since Margie's telephone equipment allowed them to leave voice-mail messages, it hadn't been a major inconvenience for them. But these were customers from whom Margie's company expected orders for a new product it had just introduced. And Margie had been asked by Bill to use every contact with these companies to promote the product.

Where was Margie?

Tim, an engineer, was a member of a new product team, and the team's leader told Bill that Tim no longer seemed a part of the group. It wasn't anything Tim said or did so much as the fact that he seemed so preoccupied with his daughter that the old camaraderie that had been critical to several major product development efforts seemed missing.

Besides, the team members had to reschedule their own work around the times when Tim was in the office, something each found extremely inconvenient. On one occasion, a meeting had had to be rescheduled when the group found that it was Tim's day to work at home.

Larry was a copywriter, and Bill continued to be pleased with his work. But Larry, who had never missed a deadline during the five years he had worked with Bill, began to miss them now—first by a day, then two days, now three.

"What have I gotten myself into?" Bill asked himself. Not only did he have to address the problem, he would have to report the experiment's progress to his boss. This would be embarrassing, since he had been so sure that Margie, Larry, and Tim would all be able to work at home successfully.

When the three arrived for their weekly progress reports, Bill asked for explanations.

Margie denied any problem; she had returned each call she had received, as well as handling the other calls that came into her line. She admitted that she hadn't had as much time over the last week to upsell, but her mother had not been feeling well and she had had to juggle the phone calls with trips to her mother's bedside when she called.

"I didn't realize your mother required that kind of attention," Bill told her. "If I had, I doubt I would have agreed to the arrangement. How do you expect to put in a full day's work at home if you have to be a nurse to your mother?"

Margie was silent. Bill told her he would have to rethink the telework. In the meantime, he suggested she consider other caregiving arrangements for her mother. It was very likely that he would have to discontinue the new work arrangement.

Tim had to admit that he was preoccupied with his daughter. It hadn't had an effect on his work, but he could understand why the new product group might think him less a member of the team. He himself had felt like he was outside looking in—out of the loop—at the last meeting. And he had to admit that he missed the give-and-take that often triggered those moments of inspiration that had led to great new products.

He actually had wanted to talk to Bill about a different arrangement—one in which he would be in the office more often, maybe a few hours each day—so that he could still be with his daughter when she needed him but also could continue to work closely with his team's members. He apologized for the inconvenience to his fellow team members of having to work around his schedule.

Larry just hung his head. He admitted that at college he had outdone his friends in procrastination, easily distracted from his studies by anything and everything. His new VCR had done him in. Friends had brought tapes, and he had been spending every day, from 9 to 9—time he should have been spending on his work—sitting in front of the television. To get his copy to Bill, he had had to work through the nights. He had just been lucky that Bill had not seen any decline in work quality, but Larry said he could see it, and it bothered him. He asked to come back to the office. Bill had suspected that Larry was sunlighting but, instead, it was a matter of poor time management.

Of the three employees in the pilot test, only one—Tim—continued to work at home, but the hours he spent interacting with his colleagues were increased to ensure better communication and to make Tim feel less isolated from the group. When the group got together other than at scheduled meetings, its members made it a point to include Tim via phone.

WIIFM

"So there are problems associated with telecommuting, you say. It's easy enough for me to deal with this problem. All I have to do is to refuse anyone who wants to work at home." Yeah? It's not so simple. More and more employees will be asking to work at home. And you may lose very talented employees who could handle telecommuting well to companies that are willing to let them prove they can handle this new work arrangement. So you need to know how to get the most out of your teleworkers.

While telecommuting might seem primarily valuable to women because of their traditional family role, men as well as women see its value in addressing work and family conflicts. This is a reflection of men's increasing assumption of traditional women's roles in families.

Flex-Place Benefits

Besides losing talented women and men by not providing telecommuting, if you refuse to accept the new arrangement you will also lose out on these benefits:

- *Greater productivity.* Surveys of executives in companies sponsoring telecommuting report an increase in productivity as well as an improvement in quality of work; they also report improved morale.

Opponents of telework argue that these higher productivity levels stem from employees' putting in more than a full day's work because there are no clear timelines. Not so, say the proponents of this new work arrangement. Productivity is higher because teleworkers are away from the distractions of the office—the phone calls, the endless meetings, and so on.

• *Greater flexibility.* Employees with special personal needs can adjust their work schedule to balance those needs with professional demands. Working hours can also reflect teleworkers' bioclocks. Morning people can begin work before the start of a regular workday, and night owls who would prefer to rise at 11 A.M. can work through the evening hours and into the night.

• *Improved time management skills.* Good telecommuters have good time management skills, and they practice them both at their home site and at the office, when they are there. They're more focused on their work, and that means that they are more likely to get done what they set out to do during a day, at home and at the office.

• *Increased customer service levels.* When phone coverage is based on individuals' bioclocks, companies can expand the hours of service, which is important to an organization that has customers in different time zones. Telework means phone coverage no matter where customers live.

• *Accessibility to talented employees.* Companies can recruit and hire talented people without paying relocation costs. They also can get employees who might otherwise not come to work for them if they had to relocate.

Ted is a well-known graphic artist living in Montgomery, New York. A design firm wanted to hire him, but it was located in New York, seventy miles away, and Ted had no wish to relocate, although he did want to work for the design firm. So Ted proposed to the firm that he telecommute. Its owner agreed, and thereafter, once a week, Ted came into the office to work with his peers. In between visits, he would phone or e-mail or fax the office.

The owner was delighted with the arrangement, particularly when one of Ted's designs got the firm a major contract with an advertising firm.

- *Reduced overhead costs.* Given the expense of office space today, telework can net considerable dollar savings. But this savings occurs only if the company can sublease or vacate space previously occupied by the teleworkers.

Telecommuting has its advantages. But it also has its problems, as is evident from Bill's experience. How can you avoid the problems and maximize the benefits of telework?

Back to the Basics

Telecommmuting has actually been around since the mid-nineteenth century, when the owner of a railroad used his company's telegraph system to manage remote divisions. But the discussion here shouldn't be about these first efforts at decentralization or later efforts at telemarketing or customer service from home, but rather about conventional management, when you have either employees working at desks just outside your own office or independent contractors who do work for your company from their homes.

The work of independent contractors has always been monitored on the basis of results. Deadlines are set for jobs, and contractors who provide quality work by the due date are likely to continue to work for you; those who don't are not given another assignment.

You can usually see how your full-time employees are doing by stepping outside your office.

Conventional Management

Smart managers don't patrol the workplace to ensure that employees are indeed keying in critical financial information, not playing computer games, or proofreading a report they have just written, not finishing the latest Ludlum novel. But they do try to be observant of employee performance to see if any problems are developing. Often, a few questions about how the job is going is enough to get an employee's mind refocused on the job and the importance of being attentive to his work.

New employees' performance is more closely monitored until their supervisor feels she can trust these hires. You don't give trust until it's earned. On the other hand, you don't consider someone guilty of inattention or of an infraction of work rules unless you have proof.

You observe work behavior to gauge those you can trust and those who need ongoing coaching and counseling. If the latter improve and periodic checks show no falloff in performance, then you are pretty safe limiting your visits to the work area to about once a week. Then you are more on the lookout for operational problems than for performance ones. Controls exist in the form of progress reports, statistical information, and perhaps one-on-one conversations between you and the employee.

Communication has always been critical. The best supervisors have always been those who have an ear open to employee needs or concerns. There has never been a time when an open door that allows employees to occasionally visit, share ideas, and maybe even vent about a situation has not been important.

Expectations about work should be clear from an employee's first day on the job. There should be no confusion about the goals or missions of the organization, because they, like the standards by which the employee will be measured, will have been discussed with the employees.

These are the building blocks of good management, and they are as relevant to managing an employee ten miles away as to supervising someone who is within your sight every day of the week.

Meet Mr. Paige: "End Trans."

To get high performance from a department, you don't have to manage like "Mr. Paige." Who's Mr. Paige? He's the boss in a movie entitled *Jumpin' Jack Flash* from the late 1980s. In it, Whoopi Goldberg plays one of several employees who handle the transfer of funds via computer in a major bank. Each morning, as Goldberg and her coworkers come into the office, where workstations are lined up, making the office seem like a modern-day sweatshop, they are watched by Mr. Paige, who stands on a raised platform. A bell sounds to mark the start of the day, and it sounds again at the end of the day. During office hours, Mr. Paige monitors the group's work from his raised platform.

Because Whoopi's character is one of his "most productive workers," he tolerates her socializing with coworkers, but on one occasion he orders her into his office to complain about her engaging in personal chitchat with data entry personnel at banks in other countries. "I just want to be friendly, Mr. Paige," Goldberg's character tells him. "Computers are not friendly," he responds. "I'm not a computer," she answers. "You will be one from nine to six," he answers. "End trans.," she concludes. Unfortunately, in the real world there are still managers like Mr. Paige. And clearly they are not the kind of manager who can handle the managerial flexibility that teleworking demands. Managing flex-place workers is no different from managing conventional workers. Good communication, clear explanations of expectations, mutually agreed-on goals and standards, and work relationships based on mutual trust are the basis for successfully managing employees within your sight, and they are also the foundation for managing flex-place workers.

Fad Solutions

Acceptance of alternative work arrangements began in the 1960s with flex-time and job sharing and even work sharing, which was an alternative to layoffs. (See the box.)

Alternative Work Arrangements

Flextime. Employees get to choose their starting and quitting times within limits set by management.

Compressed workweeks. The regular five-day workweeks are compressed into four ten-hour days, three twelve-hour days, or whatever arrangement works best for the organization.

Telecommuting (or flex-place). Work is done at home or at remote work centers connected to the company via computer, fax, and/or telephone. The remote work center
may be subsidized by the company, or it may be an independent facility where those who telecommute work because they can't deal with the distractions of home. This
is the first step to creation of virtual organizations where
all or almost all of the employees work away from the
office.

Job sharing. Two employees assume the responsibilities of
one full-time job and receive prorated salary and benefits
for doing it. There is a skill to this in that both individuals
need to be in close communication so that they can fill in
for each other.

Outsourcing. Work that might otherwise be done by an employee is contracted to someone outside the organization. Outsourcing is often used to get work previously
done by a staff member done by that same staff member
after he or she has been laid off. The company benefits
most from this arrangement. The employee still has
money coming in, but the employee loses seniority rights
and job security, fringe benefits, and maybe union membership.

Telecommuting is a combination of flex-place, flex-time,
and electronic communication. It began when one or two employees were given permission to work at home because of personal need and has grown to the point where full departments
are managed at a distance. Technology made flex-place work
possible just as the demand for off-site work from employees
grew because of new caregiving responsibilities, for a new child
or an ailing or permanently disabled parent or other member of
the family, and because of the stress associated with commuting
on overcrowded roads or trains.

There was also pressure from environmental legislation. In
1990 Congress passed the Federal Clean Air Act to identify ways
to reduce solo commuting, and telecommuting was identified as
an efficient way to comply with the ridership requirement of

the act for companies located in badly polluted regions of the country.

From the first efforts at telecommuting involving telemarketers on commission and customer service reps, it has been evident that some functions lend themselves to telework better than others. In addition to customer service and telemarketing, these include sales, writing and editing, and engineering and graphic design. All are jobs that allow management by results and do not require management by task.

Telecommuting has led to the establishment of remote work centers where telecommuters can work away from the office and nearer to home but away from the distractions of the home. Concerned about the lack of security of telecommuters from having people from various companies working together, some companies have set up centers exclusively for their employees located in remote locations where potential employees reside. These corporate centers may or may not include supervisory staff who are a part of the off-site program. For those telecommuters who complain about the loneliness of working at home, these remote work centers offer an excellent alternative.

The very newest move in flex-placing, however, is not a building but desk space that is available for drop-in staff. There are offices for core staff plus offices or sometimes just electric outlets for a laptop PC with software, cellular phone, voice mail, and electronic mail. The concept is popular in industries where employees must travel from one facility to another or for employees, such as salespersons, who do work that does not demand that they work regularly in an office. Various terms are used to describe this, including hoteling or moteling and floating offices.

Should Your Staff Telecommute?

Is telecommuting something your department can benefit from? Answer these questions to find out:

• Are office space costs going up sufficiently to justify telecommuting? Would telework make a real difference in overhead—that is, could office space be sublet, or could space

currently being used be reallocated to areas where there is anticipated growth in staff?

• Are there jobs under your supervision that could be done
more efficiently off-site than in the office? Would there be employee backlash if holders of these jobs were given the option of
working at home and other employees had to continue to work
in the office?

• Have any employees raised this issue with you yet? If so,
are they individuals you would trust to work at home? If you
agreed to their request, could you anticipate similar requests
from others?

• Would commuting be one issue that could be addressed
via telework? How about accessibility to a larger pool of employees? Would telework mean that you would have access to
skills that currently are unavailable to you because of the loca-
tion of either your company or the skilled workers?

• Can you ensure that data are kept secure? (When employees work at home or in local centers, there is a danger of
proprietary information falling into the hands of those not committed to the success of your organization.)

One of the most important considerations is whom you
allow to telecommute. You want employees who are self-motivated, self-disciplined, and experienced in the job. You want employees who have been with the company long enough to know
its policies and procedures and to be familiar with the corporate
mission and culture. You also want employees whose jobs do
not depend on regular interaction with colleagues. And as you
set specific arrangements, you want to be sure that those you
select will be able to schedule sufficient days in the office to ensure they don't feel out of the loop.

All of these issues are critical to deciding whether to approve telework for some or all workers within a department.
But little attention seems to be given to how to practice distance
management, which is the secret of successful telecommuting.

If you are used to relying mostly on observation to determine if employees are performing, shifting gears will represent
a form of culture shock. But think of it this way: Observing em-

ployees only lets you know how busy they are; it doesn't tell you about the quality of their work. To get the full picture, you also have to have ongoing communication, which is available via the new technology, regularly scheduled office visits with teleworkers, and the establishment of standards of performance that start with mutually agreed-on goals. For those whose work is linked to the computer, you might also want to install a control system that monitors efforts.

The Balancing Act

Managing telecommuters—that is, practicing distance management—really is no different from good supervision. To make a telecommuting program work in your department, all you need to do is to apply the basics of good on-site supervision to your remote employees. You supervise not via observation but on the basis of results. Your employees are managed as if they are adults who appreciate their responsibilities and can be trusted to carry them out unless they give you evidence to the contrary. You don't treat them like school students who need a room monitor to see that they behave when the teacher is called out of the room. That's what Mrs. Paige really was.

Distance management is comparable to Management by Objectives in that employees' performance is measured by the outputs of their work. Actually, companies that utilize MBO-type programs tend to have an easier time adjusting to flexible work practices because the adoption of flex-place does not represent the cultural shock it does for managers who depend on observation of behaviors for evaluations.

For this approach to work, you need to:

• *Set clear expectations.* This means that you and the employee both have to have a clear idea of what results each job is to achieve. Just as you would set key results or outcomes or standards with an on-site employee, you set these expectations with an off-site worker. Standards in both cases are in writing.

A telecommuter's agreement spells out both your organization's and the telecommuter's rights and responsibilities.

- *Agree on performance standards.* What will a good job look like? Make the measurements as quantifiable as possible. When output can't be measured in numbers, you and the remote employee need to be positive you are in agreement on what the standards mean. Again, this mirrors the process you should already be following with on-site employees.

- *Agree on how results will be monitored.* Since you can't look outside your door to see how busy your staff is, agreement on how work will be measured is critical.

What reporting methods will you use—written or verbal reports, computer tracking, phone or face-to-face meetings? How frequent will these be?

One area you'll want to monitor is Internet activity. It'll be very easy for your remote workers to become Internet junkies, caught up in the Information Highway. So include in the standards that you set what level of use will be considered an abuse of the communications technology.

- *Provide feedback on performance.* You provide ongoing feedback to your on-site employees. Do the same for your off-site employees. That feedback won't always be given in person. But it can still be provided by telephone or e-mail. If a real problem exists, you'll want to call your employee into the office for a face-to-face conversation. Actually, the means by which you provide feedback isn't as important as its frequency and how specific you can be about offering advice to improve performance.

These interim progress reports supplement traditional appraisals in which you will sit down with the remote worker and review in greater depth his performance.

- *Build trust.* Since you won't have the same control over teleworkers as you have for employees who work beside you, you have to rely on the remote control that comes from their respect in you. You can begin to foster that trust by showing that you trust them unless evidence proves that you can't. Operate on the assumption of trust, not distrust. Question only when you have real reason to do so—which is what today's outstanding supervisors do anyway, right?

- *Communicate, communicate, communicate.* I've given this advice elsewhere in this book, but nowhere is it more important than in working with remote workers. Sometimes you may have to talk to a remote worker three or four times a day. If you haven't talked to someone recently, then give him a call to see how things are going. It's the equivalent of dropping by an employee's workstation for a social chat. It tells the employee you care and gives her a chance to let you know how hard she is working.

Here's a trick you might want to use for those employees with whom communication is more often via phone than in person or through e-mail. Prepare for the meeting by developing "talking points," a list of those issues that you plan to address. You might also want the employee to e-mail or fax to you her "talking points" before the meeting. This way you are both prepared for the issues to be discussed. Time isn't wasted as one or the other of you hunts through desk files for the relevant piece of information that is being discussed.

- *Fine-tune your listening skills.* Whether the individual is in your office or on your phone, you want to give him your full attenton. Even if you could read that report while you're talking to the teleworker on the phone, put down the report and concentrate on what your employee is telling you. Show the person the respect he deserves by not doing anything else when you're on the phone with him. After all, you may discover a problem in the making or, better yet, some new source of income or operating tip that you can share with your other remote workers.

Beyond these basics, don't forget when working with teleworkers to:

- *Make access to information the same for on-site and off-site individuals.* Your on-site employees expect this; your off-site employees require it.

You want to keep communication flowing to counteract the out-of-sight, out-of-mind phenomenon that telecommuters complain about. Maybe you could develop a Web site for your team or, less complex, circulate a team newsletter through e-mail that shares the accomplishments of both remote and on-site employees and progress on tasks both groups are working on.

• *Set up technical support systems for remote workers.* What if the teleworker's computer crashes? Can she get immediate access to technical help? You'll want to work with your own systems personnel to be sure that your telecommuters have twenty-four-hour support seven days a week. (Keep in mind when you approve a request for telecommuting that your remote worker has to be knowledgeable enough about the office technology to handle most simple problems on her own and that you will likely have to contract with one or more outside service firms to address systems problems of remote workers whose computers can't be serviced by your own systems staff.)

• *Consider the reaction of staff members if not everyone is able to work at home.* Some positions still can't be handled at home—and it should be obvious which ones. But you may have to remind those employees who are upset when their request is rejected. Avoid on-site backlash by explaining the factors that influenced your decision to let one employee work at home and not another.

• *Recognize that you will need to create a sense of team even though you and all the team members aren't located in the same office.* Many of the techniques that are used to build team spirit within an on-site group can be applied to building team spirit with either an off-site group or a combined group (see Chapter 7).

If you're initiating an off-site program, you might want to begin with a meeting in which all the teleworkers and on-site staff get together physically. Use this session as an opportunity to point up the strengths of each member of the work group, those in the office and those working out of their homes. Then, over time, hold periodic group meetings, as well as send e-mail messages, to both your in-house and off-site employees in which you sing the praises of members of each group to the rest of the team.

• *Help teleworkers build camaraderie so that they will lean on one another despite the physical distance between them.* If individuals in the same neighborhood don't become pals naturally, assign each teleworker a buddy who lives nearby who can offer emotional support as well as professional help.

• *Don't be held back by the difficulty of coordinating teleworkers' visits from bringing the group together periodically to discuss operational problems.* You know how beneficial these problem-solving sessions can be with on-site employees. You can identify and address problems off-siters are experiencing or workflow between off-site and on-site employees. If travel is a problem, look into the new technology, such as audioconferences, that achieve the same result at less cost. But it's better to pay the dollars to get your group members together to talk about difficulties they are experiencing either personally or with members of your group or individuals from other groups within your organization.

While you'll want to devote a major portion of the meeting to operational issues and the group's mission, keep in mind that an equally important reason for these sessions is to get team members together. You might establish half-hour breaks in both the morning and afternoon for networking and hold a full-hour nonworking lunch. You might even want to plan a small social event in the evening to encourage more conversation among your remote workers and on-site staff.

• *Encourage teleworkers to communicate with one another as well as with you.* Encourage a little informal networking so that members of the group who are off-site stay in touch via e-mail messages not only with those in the office but with others like them who work at home.

• *Don't show favoritism to on-site employees.* You don't want to show favoritism, not even to seem to show favoritism. But where you have on-site employees as well as off-site workers, there is the danger of giving rewards and the best assignments to those in the office simply because of their presence, thereby seeming to favor your on-site workers and thereby demoralizing the at-home employees.

So think carefully before making any decisions about new assignments or recognizing work to be sure that your judgment is based on the abilities exhibited by the individuals, not on their accessibility. It's easy to think of Marge to head that special project because her desk is right outside your office, but Milton is equally qualified to do the work and can do it from home. Don, who works at home, should be recognized for anticipating a customer's needs just as much as Mary, on-site, who made sure an order was processed in time to satisfy a big account.

Make assignments and evaluate performance of both off-site and on-site workers using the same criteria. Equally important, don't show favoritism to or give the impression of showing favoritism to one off-site employee over another. Misunderstandings can arise if it seems that you spend more time on the phone or during an office visit with one teleworker than with another, just as referring to a distant team member as "that person in Buffalo" to those based in your New York headquarters suggests that Charlie, located in Buffalo, New York, isn't a member of the team. Keep in mind that perceptions, no matter how inaccurate, can destroy the trust between you and your team.

Summarizing, the secret of overseeing remote workers is to focus on the output (that is, the results), instead of on the input (e.g., ways of working, time, work space). The same applies to independent contractors. Good managers of conventional workers are good managers of remote employees, because the principles of good management work no matter the work arrangement.

Epilogue

I've been told by an educator that there is a growing belief within our business schools that we must discard entirely traditional management principles and philosophies to make the management of the nineties work effectively. After reading this book, I think you know how I would respond.

While not all traditional management is applicable in the nineties, there is much that is not yet ready to be put to pasture. Where past practices may not be directly applicable, their past use can teach us much as we attempt to move toward more productive, more creative workplaces through empowerment, shared leadership, value-laden leadership, team management, and the like.

Discarding the proven philosophies of management would make no more sense than discarding pen and pencil simply because we now have sophisticated word processors, or discontinuing mailing letters because we can now e-mail our Aunt Nellie or Uncle Dan as well as our colleagues.

Admittedly, there is a major difference between much of the management of the past and the management of the present. Whereas today's management seems more free and is designed to create more open communications and employee involvement, the management of the past, with its job descriptions, rating systems, and the like, was founded more firmly on the desire to control. But I would argue that: (1) Many managers today still micro-manage, but hide the fact by excessively using the "E" or "T" word ("empowerment" and "teamwork," for those of you who didn't really read the book and those of you who read the

Epilogue first, for whatever reason), and (2) there is nothing wrong with control per se. Indeed, if you think about the recommendations throughout this book, the balancing act often incorporates control into faddish solutions that lack critical control. Incorporating some means of controlling the new process or procedure or technique—or, if you think it has less negative connotations, "structure"—to the faddish programs and processes and principles of today can mean the difference between their successful implementation or their failure.

This book offers specific advice for practicing team management, empowerment, value-laden leadership, and a number of other concepts of the nineties. But even as it was being written, there were (and are) new buzzwords appearing in the business press: from "360-degree assessments" to "open-book management" (which has been around for a few years, but fits so perfectly into the movement toward empowering employees that it is growing in interest and application) to "tough-love supervision" (which may be the next rage in business management).

If you decide to adapt these or any other developments of the future to your workplace, keep in mind that the balancing act is as applicable to them as it is to the current issues discussed in depth in this book. But it will be up to you to find the means by which you can create the proper balance between the still-applicable basics of the past and the faddish solutions of the future. And I can help you in doing so.

In creating the most effective management blend, the most important point to keep in mind is that employees have three needs: (1) to understand what has to be accomplished, (2) to know how that outcome will be measured, and (3) to know how well he or she has done in accomplishing that result.

The decision about how the work will be accomplished can be made by the employee. So, too, can the decision about the final outcome. Measurement of the result can be assessed by either the employee, or you and the employee together. Likewise, the employee alone or you and the employee together can evaluate how well the employee has gone about accomplishing the outcome. The means is irrelevant, provided there is some structure in place to address the three needs described above.

While Tom Peters may be right in principle in cheering the

chaos of the nineties for the opportunities it offers, we practicing managers would argue that at some point there is a need for control (or structure) to ensure that the processes themselves generate the opportunities they promise and that the opportunities or outcomes are indeed achieved.

Index